GLYNDO

Volunteers

Answering the Call

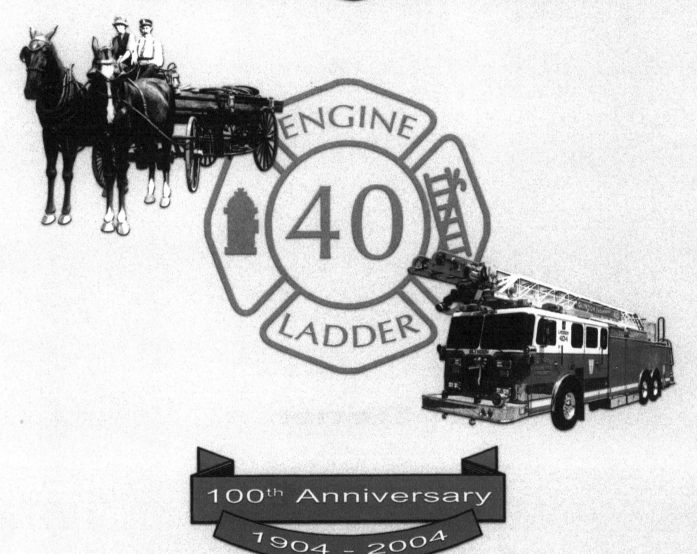

ENGINE
40
LADDER

100th Anniversary

1904 - 2004

A Centennial History
of the
Glyndon Volunteer Fire Department

Baltimore County, Maryland

TURNER PUBLISHING COMPANY
Nashville, Tennessee

Turner®
Publishing Company

www.turnerpublishing.com

Turner Publishing Company Staff:
Keith Steele: Publishing Consultant
Charlotte Harris: Project Coordinator
Susan L. Harwood, Designer

Library of Congress Control No. 2004109560

ISBN: 978-1-68162-195-1

0 9 8 7 6 5 4 3 2 1

Table of Contents

DEDICATION

One Hundred Years ago 23 dedicated citizens of the town of Glyndon recognizing the need to protect the community and its citizens from the danger of fire met together and founded the Volunteer Fire Company No. 1 of Glyndon.

For a century, this tradition of service to the community and citizens of Glyndon has been continued by the men and women of the Glyndon Volunteer Fire Department who have given, and continued to give, selflessly of their time and talent to protect their town and their neighbors.

To the Glyndon Volunteers, the men and women who have been "Answering the Call" with courage and determination for the past one hundred years we dedicate this tribute to their remarkable achievements.

Congratulatory Messages

ROBERT L. EHRLICH, JR.

GOVERNOR

STATE OF MARYLAND

STATE OF MARYLAND
OFFICE OF THE GOVERNOR

ROBERT L. EHRLICH, JR.
GOVERNOR

Dear All:

On behalf of the citizens of the State of Maryland, it is my privilege to extend to the members of The Glyndon Volunteer Fire Department my sincere congratulations on the occasion of the 100th anniversary of your founding.

One hundred years ago, a group of dedicated citizens of the town of Glyndon founded the Glyndon Volunteer Fire Company with the purpose of protecting the lives and property of their neighbors. And now, 100 years later, we celebrate their legacy of service to the Glyndon community.

Your founding members are to be gratefully remembered for their vision and selfless dedication to others. Your current members, who continue to serve without hesitation or reservation, are to be commended for the leadership they provide to Baltimore County Volunteer Firemen's Association, the Maryland State Firemen's Association, and the Baltimore County Fire Department.

I pray that all who serve in the Glyndon Volunteer Fire Department will be blessed with God's continued protection.

Best personal regards.

P.S. Thanks for all of your support over the (many) years! B

Sincerely,

Bob

Robert L. Ehrlich, Jr.
Governor

STATE HOUSE, ANNAPOLIS, MARYLAND 21401
(410) 974-3901 1-800-811-8336
TTY USERS CALL VIA MD RELAY

PAUL SARBANES
UNITED STATES SENATOR
MARYLAND

PAUL S. SARBANES
MARYLAND

United States Senate
Washington, D. C.

March 6, 2004

Glyndon Volunteer Fire Department
4812 Butler Road
P.O. Box 3671
Glyndon, Maryland 21071

Dear Friends:

I am most pleased to extend my congratulations and best wishes on the occasion of the 100th anniversary of the Glyndon Volunteer Fire Department.

It is my longstanding belief that fire fighting and EMS service are among the most demanding public service endeavors and require the very best, most dedicated efforts of those who risk their lives every day to protect and assist our citizens. For the past 100 years, the Glyndon Volunteer Fire Department has been the first line of defense against fires and other emergencies; and this anniversary celebration is indeed a tribute to your bravery, dedication, and spirit.

On this important occasion, I appreciate the opportunity to recognize the Glyndon Volunteer Fire Department on one century of service. Please accept my appreciation and very best wishes for continued success and progress in the years to come.

With best regards,

Sincerely,

Paul Sarbanes

Paul Sarbanes
United States Senator

C.A. Dutch Ruppersberger

Member of Congress

2nd District, Maryland

C.A. DUTCH RUPPERSBERGER
2ND DISTRICT, MARYLAND
MEMBER OF CONGRESS

March 4, 2004

Glyndon Volunteer Fire Company
4812 Butler Road
Glyndon, Maryland 21071

Dear Members of Glyndon Volunteer Fire Company:

Please accept my sincere congratulations on the celebration of your 100th anniversary.

I commend all of you for the volunteer time you devote to protecting the lives of the citizens in the communities you so ably serve. As volunteers, you make up a large part of the "first responder team" and play a large role in homeland security.

As the former County Executive and now as the Congressman representing a portion of the Glyndon area, it is my honor and privilege to pay tribute to you on this great occasion.

Sincerely,

Dutch

C.A. Dutch Ruppersberger

Not Printed at Government Expense

Dan K. Morhaim

Bobby A. Zirkin

Jon S. Cardin

Maryland House of Delegates

THE MARYLAND HOUSE OF DELEGATES
ANNAPOLIS, MARYLAND 21401-1991

The Glyndon Volunteer Fire Company

March 6, 2004

The Baltimore County, District 11 Delegation wishes to congratulate you on the 100th Anniversary of continued service to your community. This milestone recognizes your dedication to the safety and well being of not only your community, but your friends and family as well. A volunteer fire company exists at the discretion of local community involvement, and this achievement is a shining example of what is best in your community.

At this time, we are pleased to recognize your 100 years of service with an Official Citation from the Baltimore County, District 11 Delegation.

We wish you continued success in your volunteer capacity. If we can be of any assistance to you, please do not hesitate to contact our office.

Sincerely,

Dan K. Morhaim
Delegate, District 11

Bobby A. Zirkin
Delegate, District 11

Jon S. Cardin
Delegate, District 11

James T. Smith

County Executive

Baltimore County, Maryland

James T. Smith, Jr.
Baltimore County Executive

Executive Office
400 Washington Avenue, Towson, Maryland 21204
Tel: 410-887-2450 • Fax: 410-887-4049

Baltimore County

One of the Best-Managed Counties in America

July 25, 2003

Dear Glyndon Volunteer Fire Company:

It is with great pleasure that I congratulate you on your organization's 100 years of service to the Glyndon community.

Baltimore County's neighborhoods have withstood tremendous change over the past century. Unlike many institutions that have not been able to transition from decade to decade, volunteer fire companies, such as yours, have shown tremendous resilience. Not only are you an essential part of our emergency service, but you are also key to the vitality of our older, more mature communities.

The citizens of Glyndon depend on you to meet their emergency needs. While these needs have changed over the years, they have not diminished. Please know how much I appreciate your dedication to the fire department and your commitment to the community.

On behalf of the people of Baltimore County, best wishes for a wonderful anniversary celebration and for many more years of service.

Sincerely,

James T. Smith Jr.
County Executive

Visit the County's Website at www.baltimorecountyonline.info

T. Bryan McIntire

Councilman, Third District

Baltimore County, Maryland

County Council of Baltimore County
Court House, Towson, Maryland 21204

T. Bryan McIntire
Councilman, Third District

Council Office: 410-887-3387
Facsimile: 410-887-5791

March 6, 2004

Edward C. Schultz, President
Glyndon Volunteer Fire Department
4812 Butler Road
Glyndon, Maryland 21071

Dear Ted:

I am delighted to have the opportunity to write to you on the occasion of the 100th anniversary of the Glyndon Volunteer Fire Department. It has been said that the longest journey begins with the first step and that first step was taken on March 4, 1904 when a group of local residents met in Townsend Hall and decided to form a volunteer fire company for the Glyndon community. In June of that year the organizers had a fundraiser and raised $300 which was matched by an equal donation from the County Commissioners thus raising $600.00 which equates to $12,000 in 2003. With money in hand, the company purchased and took delivery in December of 1904 of a hook and ladder truck with a gold pump that was horse drawn.

From these meager beginnings, a spirit of dedication and determination of its founding fathers has been carried forward by their successors. Many obstacles and challenges along the way have been overcome. Today the department occupies its firehouse originally constructed in 1956 and is well equipped with one engine, one ladder truck, a modern utility vehicle and a special unit.

Throughout its 100 years, the Glyndon Volunteer Fire Department has served the Glyndon community and Baltimore County with distinction and it is with gratitude and thankfulness that I offer sincere congratulations on the occasion of its 100th anniversary.

Sincerely,

Bryan McIntire

T. Bryan McIntire
Councilman, Third District

TBM:dlm
schultz 100th ann.ltr.wpd

Chief John J. Hohman
Baltimore County
Fire Department

Baltimore County
Fire Department

700 East Joppa Road
Towson, Maryland 21286-5500
410-887-4500

July 17, 2003

Glyndon Volunteer Fire Department
4812 Butler Road
P.O. Box 3671
Glyndon, MD 21071

To the Members of The Glyndon Volunteer Fire Department:

Congratulations on the 100th anniversary of your fire company! It's hard to imagine what it must have been like in 1904, when the company was founded with humble beginnings and big dreams. Since then, your apparatus, tools, and station house have undergone many transformations to modernize and keep up with technology. What hasn't changed since 1904 is the members' commitment to Glyndon and its surrounding communities. There are few institutions that people care about enough to support for more than a few decades, but you, the Glyndon Volunteers, have shown the fortitude to last a full century—with no sign of stopping! Enjoy your celebration this year and best of luck in your next century of activity.

Sincerely,

John J. Hohman
Fire Chief

Visit the County's Website at www.baltimorecountyonline.info

Printed with Soybean Ink on Recycled Paper

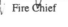

Joel C. McCrea, President Baltimore County Volunteer Firemen's Association

THE
BALTIMORE COUNTY
VOLUNTEER
FIREMEN'S ASSOCIATION
Public Safety Building
700 East Joppa Road
Towson, MD 21286-5500
Phone: (410) 887-4885
Fax: (410) 887-4852
www.bcvfa.org

MEMBER COMPANIES

Arbutus Volunteer Fire Co.
Arcadia Volunteer Fire Co.
Boring Volunteer Fire Co.
Bowley's Quarters Vol. Fire Co.
Box 234 Association
Butler Volunteer Fire Co.
Central Alarmers Association
Chestnut Ridge Volunteer. Fire Co.
Cockeysville Volunteer Fire Co.
Cowenton Volunteer Fire Co.
English Consul Volunteer Fire Co.
Glyndon Volunteer Fire Co.
Hereford Volunteer EMS/Rescue Co.
Hereford Volunteer Fire Co.
Hyde Park Volunteer Fire Co.
Jacksonville Volunteer Fire Co.
Kingsville Volunteer Fire Co.
Lansdowne Volunteer Fire Co.
Liberty Road Volunteer Fire Co.
Long Green Volunteer Fire Co.
Lutherville Volunteer Fire Co.
Maryland Line Volunteer Fire Co.
Middleborough Volunteer Fire Co.
Middle River Volunteer Fire Co.
Middle River Vol. Res. Ambulance Co.
North Point-Edgemere Vol. Fire Co.
Owings Mills Volunteer Fire Co.
Pikesville Volunteer Fire Co.
Providence Volunteer Fire Co.
Reisterstown Volunteer Fire Co.
Rockaway Beach Volunteer Fire Co.
Rosedale Volunteer Fire Co.
Violetville Volunteer Fire Co.
Wise Avenue Volunteer Fire Co.
Woodlawn Volunteer Fire Co.

AFFILIATIONS

NFPA MEMBER

March 4, 2004

Officers and Members
Glyndon Volunteer Fire Department
4812 Butler Road
Glyndon, Maryland 21071

Dear Fellow Firefighters:

It is with the greatest of pleasure that I write to you now, just one hundred years from the day your company was founded. On behalf of the thirty-five member companies of the Association, and their three thousand five hundred members we offer our congratulations upon completion of a century of dedicated service.

Not only has the Glyndon Volunteer Fire Department diligently protected the lives and property of Glyndon and the surrounding neighborhood, it has provided leadership for volunteer fire fighters around the county. A Founding Member of this Association, six of its members have served honorably as our president.

Its volunteer firefighters, rescue and emergency medical service providers are a glorious American tradition. WE wish you the best of everything, as you continue that tradition into your second century of service!

Sincerely,

Joel C. McCrea

Joel C. McCrea
President

Terry E. Thompson, President
Maryland State
Firemen's Association

MARYLAND STATE FIREMEN'S ASSOCIATION

Representing the Volunteer Fire, Rescue, and Emergency Services Personnel

TERRY E. THOMPSON
President 2003-2004
6122 Tulane Drive
Clarksville, Maryland 21029
H (410) 531 - 3342
Fax (301) 776 - 0024
Pager (410) 313 - 0021
e-mail: tthompson@msfa.org

To the Members of the Glyndon Volunteer Fire Co., Inc.

On behalf of the Maryland State Firemen's Association, I would like to congratulate you as you celebrate your 100th anniversary.

The members should be proud of this great achievement. It is an honor to reach this milestone. Let's not forget your founding fathers that saw the need for a fire department to serve the citizens in the Glyndon area.

We wish you success in the years to come and hope that you will be able to continue with this great volunteer tradition to your community.

Once again, congratulations and may God bless you and protect you as you protect the citizens of your community.

Sincerely,

Terry

Terry E. Thompson
President, MSFA

HEADQUARTERS THIRD CORPS AREA
UNITED STATES ARMY
OFFICE OF THE CORPS AREA COMMANDER
BALTIMORE, MARYLAND

March 29, 1928.

The Chief of the Fire Department,
Glyndon, Maryland.

My dear Chief:

This is just a note to express my sincere thanks for the prompt and efficient service rendered by your unit during the fire at my house on March 27th. It was the type of prompt civic service that I shall not soon forget, and I am deeply appreciative to you all.

Sincerely yours,

DOUGLAS MacARTHUR,
Major General, U. S. Army.

Preface

In this book, the members of the Glyndon Volunteer Fire Department chronicle the courage and sacrifices of the many men and women who have, over the last 100 years, worked and given selflessly of themselves to build an organization dedicated to the protection of their friends and neighbors. It starts with the history of our town and the fire that galvanized the citizens of Glyndon and motivated them to form the Volunteer Fire Company No.1 of Glyndon.

The story of 100 years of dedication and hard work, beginning with a single piece of apparatus drawn by livery horses and stored in a borrowed shed, and culminating in the plans for our second century is told through the words and deeds of our members and officers. From time to time, over the years, a broader history has impacted the department. Two world wars, Korea, Vietnam, and now September 11, 2001 and the war on terrorism that has come in its wake have had, and continue to have, a significant effect on the department and its members. We have included these events and how they have affected us in our story. A century of fire apparatus, the Ladies Auxiliary, and our Junior Fire Department are all important to the story of Glyndon Volunteer Fire Department and they have their place in this volume. We celebrate our members and our officers, and the pride we all have in our department on these pages.

In a letter received from the late General Douglas MacArthur, he refers to "prompt and efficient service" and commends the department for "prompt civic service" . These are the reasons why 23 men met in March of 1904 to provide their neighbors with "prompt and efficient service." They saw it as their "civic duty." It is the reason why the over 80 men and women of the Glyndon Volunteer Fire Department serve their community today.

In the final analysis, it all comes down to our dedicated people and the generous support of our community, and that's the story we tell here.

Glyndon's History

GLYNDON – FOUNDED 1871

No history of the Glyndon Volunteer Fire Department would be complete without an understanding of the origins of the town of Glyndon. Events in the town's history had a direct impact on the decision by a group of its citizens to organize a volunteer fire company to protect the people and property of the town.

Glyndon celebrated its 100th anniversary in 1971. The chronicling of the rise of the new town of Glyndon in 1871 is wonderfully detailed in the 100th anniversary publication by the Glyndon Community Association titled " The Glyndon Story 1871 - 1971" by Myrtle S. Eckhardt. The Association has graciously given the Glyndon Volunteer Fire Department permission to use excerpts from this excellent publication to set the scene for the organization of the "Volunteer Fire Company No. 1 of Glyndon" in 1904.

THE GLYNDON SITE

The Western Maryland Railroad promoted the early location and growth of the town of Glyndon. After the railroad reached Owings Mills by August of 1850, the plan of General Latrobe, the surveyor, called for its extension through Reisterstown and on to Westminster. However, the Reisterstown people refused to sell the right of way, and the route was changed to come through Gwynnbrook, St. Georges, and the present site of Glyndon to Emory Grove. This was completed in 1860. The railroad reached Westminster on June 15, 1861.

This new route came through an area that was beautiful, with green expanses and tall trees, and with an elevation above sea level of almost 700 feet, making delightful summers and mild winters. The eastern edge of the Glyndon site overlooked Worthington Valley where, prior to 1850, the Worthington, Longnecker, Geist and other families had established large estates. A dirt road from the valley stretched through future Glyndon to connect with the Hanover, Westminster and Baltimore turnpikes, where stagecoach roads had invited greater numbers of people to settle.

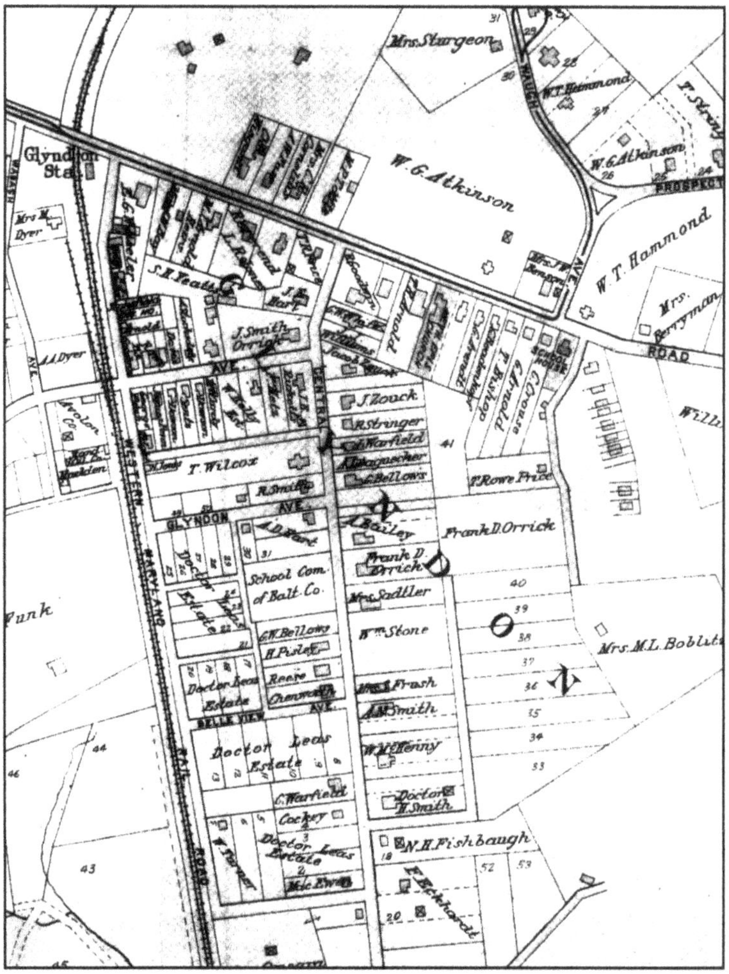

Bromley's map of Glyndon from the 1915 Atlas of Baltimore County. (Courtesy of BCPL)

PLANS FOR THE TOWN

Prior to 1871, Dr. Charles A. Leas, of Baltimore, had bought a large farm comprising most of the southern half of Glyndon, with the present O'Meara property as the nucleus. He had been appointed, in 1854, the first health officer of Baltimore City, and in subsequent years, was sent by the President of the United States as American consul to Sweden, Norway, Madeira, and British Honduras. He now wanted to retire from active city life. A news writer for the Sun of February 13, 1952, states, "He soon found that running a farm was not his métier, so he decided to found a little town, where he could live amongst congenial people of his own tastes and inclinations."

He bought additional land to the north from Robert H. Pennington, employed the Baltimore surveyor, Augustus Bouldin, and planned the town with streets, planting rows of maple trees along them. Mr. George Arnold, who was until his death, the oldest living member in our town and our town historian, sets 1871 as the year this was begun.

The name of Glyndon does not appear in the 1877 Atlas of Baltimore County, and the station

View of Railroad Avenue showing Townsend Hall and Kelly's Blacksmith Shop. (Courtesy of BCPL)

(Above) The original Glyndon Railroad Depot built in 1895 and destroyed by fire in 1903. The building was made of Texas marble with a red tile roof. (Courtesy of BCPL)

(Below) The present Glyndon Railroad Station built on the site of the original Depot in 1904. The building currently houses the U.S. Post Office for Glyndon. (GVFD Photo)

location is called Reisterstown Station. People were not satisfied with this name, for Reisterstown was almost two miles away. Mr. Bouldin suggested to Dr. Leas that the residents of the town place names in a hat and have a public drawing. John M. Hood, president of the Western Maryland Railroad, attended the drawing and a member of his family drew the Scotch name, "Glyn," from which the name "Glyndon" was coined. Both town and railroad station were so-named in 1879, according to the railroad records and to our own historian.

Other Small Business Ventures

"Railroad Avenue seems to have been the "business section" of the town. Next to Townsend Hall in the 1890s, Charles Kelly built the blacksmith shop, with shop in the end next to the hall and a wheelwright shop two stories high at the southern end, operated by Benjamin Stansfield...."

"The livery stable, conveniently located next to the blacksmith shop, was built by Charles S. Smith in the 1890s....Hanson Rutter took over the livery stable when he purchased the corner house on Chatsworth Avenue. The State Roads building (was) on the site of the old livery stable."

"Benjamin Stansfield's sons built there own wheelwright shop on Railroad Avenue between the.... (site of the)....State Roads Garage and the old fire engine house...."

These short excerpts from the "Story of Glyndon" by Myrtle S. Eckhardt describes a number of the Glyndon businesses that played an important role in the early history of the Fire Company. The company was organized and met in Townsend Hall. The horses used to pull the Hook and Ladder were supplied by Rutters Livery Stable. The Stansfield Brothers were engaged to help build the first motorized fire engine owned by the company. Chas. Kelly was engaged to provide blacksmith services to the company. These men were also active members of the fledgling company.

The Railroad Station

In 1895, the Western Maryland authorities built a station of Texas marble on the present site with a red tile roof, considered the most beautiful one along the entire line. James J. O'Meara, a stonecutter from Baltimore furnished the stone for the building. In 1903, however, when John Dyer was the agent, the station was destroyed by fire in spite of the valiant efforts of the "bucket brigade" to save it.

The Fire that Started it All

The headlines from the Baltimore American of December 25, 1903 tell the story of the disastrous fire that destroyed the Glyndon Depot

The Baltimore American goes on to tell us that the fire started at about 2:30 in the afternoon. The telegraph operator and station agent Mr. John J. Dyer discovered the fire and "raised the cry of fire" and notified the Western Maryland Railroad and the Pikesville Volunteer Fire Company. The Pikesville Company sent men and equipment to the Glyndon Depot fire on a railroad car provided by the Western Maryland Railroad.

FIRE DESTROYS GLYNDON DEPOT

WESTERN MARYLAND RAILROAD STATION WRECKED.

Damage Between $10,000 and $12,000, Covered by Insurance — Fire Is Supposed to Have Been Caused by Overheated Furnace Pipe — Apparatus From Pikesville Hurried to the Scene on a Railroad Car— Heroic Efforts to Save Some of the Movable Property.

The Western Maryland Station at Glyndon, Baltimore county, was completely wrecked by fire yesterday afternoon. The damage is estimated at between $10,000 and $12,000, and is fully covered by insurance.

The cause of the fire is not known, but it is conjectured that one of the pipes of the hot-air furnace became overheated and burst, setting fire to surrounding woodwork, as the base of the blaze was near the furnace.

Shortly after half past 2 o'clock in the afternoon, Mr. John J. Dyer, the telegraph operator, and station agent, discovered smoke coming from the basement, and upon investigating discovered that the section of the cellar near the hot-air furnace was ablaze. He immediately raised the cry of "Fire," after which he telegraphed to the railroad company, and notified the Pikesville Volunteer Fire Company by telephone.

Clipping from The Baltimore American December 25, 1903. (BCPL Files)

The Sun paper also reported on the fire in its December 25, 1903 edition. This account indicates that a request was made by the railroad for a chemical engine from the Arlington fire station. This was a Baltimore County Fire Department station located on Reisterstown Road near Belvedere Avenue. The station became part of Baltimore City in 1919. The railroad sent an engine and a car with 25 men to take the chemical engine to Glyndon. The permission of the Fire Marshall was required for the apparatus to respond but he could not be found so the engine remained in its station.

Twenty members of the Pikesville Volunteer Fire Company boarded a car at the Sudbrook station "taking their ladders, buckets, hand extinguishers, and a lever pump with hose." The train arrived in Glyndon at 3:45, the10 mile trip from Pikesville having been made in 12 minutes! The fire had been burning for an hour when they arrived and by this time the roof had fallen in and the station was essentially lost. The Pikesville firefighters then "turned every effort" to preventing the spread of the fire to adjoining structures. Water was in short supply and a nearby well was pumped dry by the Pikesville firefighters. The water supply for the station was in the cellar of the building and was therefore not available for fire fighting. It should be noted that 20 members of the Pikesville Company responded to the Glyndon Depot fire and that this crew was available at 2:30 in the afternoon on a Thursday, which was also Christmas Eve!

Great credit needs to be given to the citizens of Glyndon who rushed to the station and removed baggage, furniture, records and the like from the station saving them from the fire. The fire was in the cellar and the volunteers from the community worked at removing valuables from the station until the fire broke through the floor.

A new station was built on the same site in 1904. The new building is of a more conservative architectural design and does not reflect the grandeur of the building it replaced. The building currently houses the U.S. Post Office for Glyndon.

The Baltimore American reported on the aftermath of the fire. "After the fire temporary quarters were taken in the Dyer Building opposite the depot, and a set of telegraph equipment will be installed this morning" The Baltimore American report continues, "The residents of Glyndon are in a stir over the lack of fire protection in the vicinity, the Pikesville Company, ten miles distant, being the most convenient fire fighting organization."

The Great Baltimore Fire of February 1904 significantly influenced the decision to form a Fire Company at Glyndon. (Courtesy of The Maryland Historical Society, Baltimore Maryland)

The fire that destroyed the Glyndon Railroad Depot in December of 1903 was followed all too quickly, in February of 1904, by the Great Baltimore Fire. As had been reported, the citizens of Glyndon were already deeply concerned with the lack of fire protection for their town. This second disastrous fire, coming just months after the loss of the Depot had a significant effect on the citizens of Glyndon. Action by the town's leaders came quickly with a meeting of the community being held on March 4, 1904 for the purpose of discussing fire protection for the town. This was "A call to Serve." The rest is history, 100 years of service to Glyndon and the surrounding community.

Our History

ANSWERING THE CALL
1904 - 2004

J. Peter Brach, Jr.

A meeting of a group of residents was called on March 4, 1904 to discuss fire protection for the town of Glyndon. It was at this meeting held in Townsend Hall, later known as Redmen's Hall, that it was decided to form a volunteer fire company for the Glyndon Community. In accordance with action taken at that meeting the Volunteer Fire Company No. 1 of Glyndon was formally organized at a second meeting held on March 25, 1904. The minutes of the second meeting show the following twenty-three men as active members:

J. Smith Orrick, Chas. R. McNeal, J. J. Dyer, T. R. Arnold, G. H. Taylor, Chas. E. Sentz, Wm. Chineworth, Geo. A. Schull, C. H. Whittle, G. G. Dausser, A. A. Rich, W. T. Stringer, C. C. Billmyer, Chas. B. Kelly, Geo. E. Smith, J. H. Lohr, Chas. Switzer, A. M. Ruby, D. Danner, Henry Baublitz, Ernest Benson, Albert Henry and T. Whittle.

The following first officers were elected at this meeting: President, J. Smith Orrick; 1st Vice President, Chas. R. McNeal; 2nd Vice President, J. J. Dyer; Secretary, W. T. Stringer; Treasurer, T. Reese Arnold; Ass't. Secretary, C. C. Billmyer; Chief Foreman, Geo. H. Taylor; 1st Ass't. Foreman, Chas. B. Kelly; 2nd Ass't. Foreman, Chas. E. Sentz; Marshal, Wm. Chineworth; Ass't. Marshal, Geo. A. Schull; Librarian, C. H. Whittle; Janitor, Grover C. Danner.

In November of 1904 the By – Laws of the company were amended to change the name of the company from the Volunteer Fire Company No. 1 of Glyndon to the Glyndon Volunteer Fire Company. This name appears on the first papers of incorporation filed in March of 1905. A later incorporation changed the company name again to the Glyndon Volunteer Fire Department.

Regular meetings to conduct the business of the company were held the first and third Thursday of each month. In July of 1907 the regular meetings were changed to the second and fourth Thursday of each month. In May of 1917 it was decided that the business of the company required weekly meetings, and the company elected to meet every Monday night.

With the business of organization taken care of, the company turned to the matter of acquiring a piece of fire fighting apparatus. On April 13, 1904, a committee appointed by the President visited the County Commissioners to seek their assistance in the purchase of a piece of apparatus for the fledging company.

Mr. T. Reese Arnold reported that after thoroughly explaining the needs and objectives of the new fire company, the Commissioners agreed to match whatever money the company could raise up to $300.00. With this promise in hand, plans were made immediately to raise funds for the purchase of a piece of apparatus. An entertainment committee of firemen was appointed to organize a Bazaar and Play for this worthy cause. The President appointed the following men to this committee: W. O. Heltobridle, W. T. Stringer, G. C. Danner, C. H. Whittle and H. Lohr.

In June of 1904 a Bazaar and Entertainment was held at the Glyndon Park Auditorium. A gross profit of $162.88 was shown with expenses of $40.30. A net profit of $122.58 was realized from the affair. In July of 1904, a special subscription by the residents of the community raised $110.00. An Oyster Supper showed a profit of $84.78

With fund raising for the proposed apparatus underway, the secretary of the company was instructed to communicate with Mr. Herrman, then Fire Marshal of Baltimore County, to ascertain the first steps to be taken towards the purchase of apparatus, and what could be purchased for about $600.00.

The matter of a fire alarm was also considered, and the following article was added to the constitution governing its use of the alarm bell. Article 8- "The Bell."

Section 1 - The Bell shall be sounded as follows; in case of fire the first member at the house shall strike the bell rapidly a definite number of times which shall constitute an alarm of fire.

Section 2 - The sound of a fire alarm being productive of uncalled for fears and excitement on the part of the citizens, the members, therefore, are warned against willingly committing such an offense under the penalty of expulsion.

Section 3 - The sounding of the Bell for unusual meetings of the members shall only be done by direction of the majority of the standing committee through the President or in his absence, one of the Vice Presidents respectively.

A motion was made by Mr. Chineworth that a bell be procured. The motion was submitted to the Standing Committee. There is no record of any action being taken on the motion.

In the months following the visit to the commissioners, a committee had been investigating the purchase of a piece of apparatus for the company. During this investigation they had visited A. B. Whitlock Company of Baltimore who at the time were making a Hook and Ladder truck. Mr. A. B. Whitlock attended the meeting of the company held on September 15, 1904 to submit plans and specifications for a "Hook and Ladder" apparatus. A discussion was also held with Mr. Whitlock "as to pumps and their capacities." At this time, a motion was made by Mr. Chineworth to submit the plans and specifications to the "Standing Committee." The motion was passed.

A committee composed of Mr. Arnold, Mr. Kelly, Mr. G. H. Taylor, Mr. A. M. Ruby and Mr. C. Sentz was appointed to investigate the apparatus proposed by A. B. Whitlock of Baltimore to determine if " in their judgment" it was "suitable for our purpose," "and the price can be made satisfactory." Mr. Ruby reported for the committee at the November 3, 1904 meeting of the company indicating that the committee was "satisfied with the apparatus and that their (the A. B. Whitlock Company) offering is suited to the purposes of the company." Mr. C. H. Whittle moved, and Mr. Danner seconded, that the report be approved. Mr. Whittle's motion was amended by Mr. McNeal to approve the report and to contract for the "machine." Mr. Arnold further amended the motion by moving that the committee be empowered to "purchase the Machine" if "satisfactory terms can be made" and that the President be empowered to sign the contract. Mr. Ruby seconded this latest version of the motion to purchase the company's first piece of apparatus.

1904 A. B. Whitlock Hook and Ladder. On the apparatus (L to R) Elmer Davis and William Roylston. Horses belonging to Hans Rutter. (GVFD Archives, photo restored by Westinghouse Electric Corp, 1964)

With their specification and plans, the approval of the committee, the company, and the approval of a Mr. Herrman, the Fire Marshal of Baltimore County, they ordered the A. B. Whitlock Hook and Ladder truck with a Gould pump for approximately $600.00. This truck was delivered in December of 1904. The Hook and Ladder truck was horse drawn and answered fire alarms with horses supplied by Rutter's Livery Stable.

Some problems arose with the new apparatus. The pump was working "very unsatisfactorily" and the ladder also was not working properly. A letter was sent to A. B. Whitlock regarding the problems with the pump and the ladder. The problems were solved in good order by the A. B. Whitlock Company. The manufacturer of the

Gould pump sent a representative who determined that a new foot valve was required. The bill for the apparatus was presented to the company at the February 2, 1905 meeting and paid.

With the new apparatus in service, and having raised $393.52 toward its purchase, the President and Vice President visited the County Commissioner in January of 1905 to seek the aid that had been promised months before. The County Commissioners, it is reported, immediately gave them a check for the $300.00 they had agreed to provide. The Commissioners also pointed out that they could provide no additional assistance at that time.

Considerable discussion was held on the matter of a building to house the apparatus and serve as a fire station for the Glyndon community. At this time the equipment was being stored at the Glen Morris Supply Building. In February of 1905 a committee approached Mr. Goodwin on selling his lot on Railroad Avenue for no more than $300.00. Mr. Goodwin told the committee he did not care to sell the lot at that time. Later that month the committee reported that Mr. Kelly had bought a piece of property on Railroad Avenue known as the Smith lot and would sell a portion of the property to the company. The Smith lot was 52 feet wide and 175 feet deep. Mr. Kelly advised the company that he would sell part of the lot for $125.00. After discussion it was decided that a lot with 25 front feet and 87-1/2 feet deep would suffice for the engine house. It was moved by Mr. Arnold, and seconded by Mr. Ruby, to purchase the property for $125.00 and that the Treasurer send Mr. Kelly a check for $25.00 to "bind the price." It is interesting to note that Mr. Ruby indicated to the company at a meeting in November of 1904, that purchasing Townsend Hall (Redmen's Hall) would be a good investment. There is no record of any serious effort to purchase this building. The hall was used frequently by the company for its meetings in the years prior to the construction of the engine house on Railroad Avenue and this may account for the interest in the building. The building, known later as Redmen's Hall, was razed on January 20, 1970. Kelly's Blacksmith Shop was razed on the previous day, January 19, 1970. The demolition of these buildings brought to a close a chapter in the early history of the department.

With the business of the company moving ahead rapidly it was decided that the company should incorporate. The original charter of the organization was drawn up, free of charge, by Mr. Rich and filed in March of 1905.

Having acquired the lot on Railroad Avenue, a committee was appointed in March of 1905 to draw up specifications and plans to erect a building on this property. This committee comprised of the following members: C. R. McNeal, H. E. Rutter, W. T. Stringer, C. E. Sentz and C. C. Billmyer and was known as the "Moonlight Committee."

At the March 16, 1905 meeting, a special committee was appointed consisting of: W. T. Stringer, J. Pfeiffer and H. E. Rutter, to solicit money for an alarm bell.

On June 15,1905, the building committee reported to the company that they had sent out plans and received bids on the proposed building. The bids submitted were opened and were as follows: S. G. Marshall, $1,150.00, G. Walter Tovel, $1,150.00; John McEwin, $1,486.00. Not having sufficient funds to erect a building of the type planned, the building was tabled for the time being.

The first recorded report of a fire alarm was on July 19, 1905, at the Culbreath Farm. The Foreman reported that the apparatus was gotten out and hurried to the fire until stopped halfway being informed that it was not necessary to proceed. The fire had been put out by the farm hands. The Foreman further reported than in addition to himself, Mr. Rutter and a third man responded with the apparatus. It was estimated that the apparatus could have reached the fire in fifteen minutes from the time of alarm.

On October 5, 1905, Mr. Arnold reported for the Standing Committee a recommendation that "as the company was not in a position to erect a building on the plans suggested that the company proceed forthwith with the erection of a building at a cost of $600.00 to $650.00." A new committee was appointed to investigate construction of a building for an engine house. A motion was made by Mr. Chineworth to accept the report and to authorize the committee to proceed on a building costing $600.00 to $700.00.

A motion was made to purchase fifteen red sweaters for the company at about $.75 each. These sweaters would be sold to the members for $.25 with the company making up the difference. The motion was tabled after considerable "argument."

In November of 1905, it was brought to the attention of the committee that the Hook and Ladder truck then stored in the Glen Morris Supply Building was being eaten up and destroyed by the fertilizer being stored on one side of the truck and the horse stable on the other. Mr. William Kingsbury offered his shed to store the apparatus. The Hook and ladder was not immediately moved to the shed as it was too short and the ladders would have to be removed in order to fit the apparatus in the building. After considerable discussion the committee was ordered to remove the ladders temporarily and move the apparatus "at once." The truck was then moved to the Kingsbury Wagon Shed which was later a State Highway Administration garage. The building has been razed and a local park constructed on the site by Baltimore County.

State Roads Garage. Original Fire House is seen to far right. (Courtesy BCPL)

The company elected to join the Maryland State Firemen's Association in May of 1906. In August of 1907 a letter was received from the Towson Fire Department, then a volunteer company, requesting a delegation from the company to attend a special meeting at Towson on August 20th. The purpose of this meeting was to organize the Baltimore County Volunteer Firemen's Association. A second meeting was held on September 20, 1907, at the Junker Hotel in Baltimore. At this meeting the association was formally organized and officers elected. The Glyndon Volunteer Fire Company was one of the original fourteen companies forming the Baltimore County Volunteer Firemen's Association.

In August of 1907, a committee composed of President J. Smith Orrick, Secretary Harry E. Goodwin and Chas. B. Sentz was given authority to contract for the erection of the building for the new engine house. The new "Truck House" as it was known then was finally completed on the Railroad Avenue property in January of 1908. The fire apparatus was moved from the Kingsbury Shed to its new quarters and on January 30, 1908, the first meeting was held at the new Truck House using a stove, desk and chairs donated by the members of the company. This structure was in use by the company until the present building was occupied in 1956. The building, located at 41 Railroad Avenue, is still standing and is presently occupied by Spedo UK Ltd., a manufacturer of mailing room equipment.

County Park on site of old State Roads Garage. (GVFD Photo)

The company decided to send its truck and delegation to the County Association Convention in Towson in April of 1908. It was further decided that the delegates should be in uniform. It was decided to purchase a white cap with a black band, a blue shirt, a black belt and white gloves. The total cost of these first uniforms was $.90.

In the short space of four years this young fire company had become a fully organized operating fire department with a modern piece of apparatus and a new building to house it. They had helped to organize the County Firemen's Association and had become deeply involved in the affairs of the State Firemen's Association. This remarkable progress is a tribute to the civic interest and energy of the original twenty-three members and the many who became members in these early years.

Original Engine House completed in January 1908. 1937 Ford and 1947 Mack apparatus can be seen in the doorway. (GVFD Archives)

Unfortunately, the company records do not contain any record of the early fire alarms that the company responded to and because of this an interesting facet of the history of the fire company has been lost.

However, a fire of conflagration proportions occurred in Glyndon on September 6, 1910 and was reported in the *Baltimore Sun* of September 7, 1910. The fire all but destroyed Glyndon Park, the first prohibition camp in Maryland. The *Sun* reported that the fire started in the kitchen of a cottage owned by a Mr. Heath. "Mrs. Heath had lighted a burner under an oven and had gone to meet a friend at the [trolley] car line. The baby was out with the maid and nobody was in the cottage when the fire started." Overflowing oil from the stove is believed to have started the fire. "Roszell Cook, of the Glyndon Fire Company discovered the fire. He was delivering groceries and when he saw the blaze he ran to the store of B. W. Pindell, where he is employed, and Mr. Pindell telephoned the alarm." The alarm of fire was sounded by the bell on the firehouse by Hans Rutter, a member of the company. The *Sun* reports that every member of the fire company responded to the fire alarm as did a number of people in Reisterstown who heard the commotion and rushed to the scene of the fire.

"Mr. Charles E. Sentz, Chief [Foreman] of the company ran from his grocery store and, with the assistance of other members of the company, dragged the engine, which is equipped with a hand pump manned by four men, to the park." There is no mention in the *Sun's* account of the horses from Rutter's livery that were normally used to pull the engine. On arrival, they found the Heath cottage was a "pile of ashes." The cottage of the Aged Peoples Outing Association (A. P. O. A.) that adjoined the Heath cottage was also lost. By the time the firefighters arrived the fire had spread and a number of buildings were in flames. Using the hand pump, water was pumped from a well on the property. The well's water supply was not sufficient to supply the fire fighting efforts and was pumped dry a number of times. The hose available on the Glyndon engine was not long enough to reach other wells on the property. A two-wheeled chemical engine belonging to Mr. William A. Trottle was brought to the scene by Steven Logers, an African American employee of Mr. Trottle. This apparatus "was effective in supplementing the meager water supply."

"Every available man co-operated with the volunteer firemen," reports the *Sun*, "but their zeal was equaled by a number of young women who formed a bucket brigade and passed buckets to the men." Mrs. Alice Pollock, Misses Grace Bennett, Eilleen McKenney, Bessie Gore, Mary Shago, Marie Gore, Hellen Bennett and Susie Harris are mentioned in the *Sun's* account as participating in the firefighting efforts. The citizens of Glyndon also responded to save the furniture and belongings from the threatened cottages.

1912 hand drawn Chemical Engine with members of the Glyndon Junior Fire Company. (L to R) R. Granville, N. Baublitz, Robert Davis, George Bowers, Howard Arendt, Robert Martin, Fred Tome and J. Edward Hewes. (GVFD Archives)

High winds and dry conditions hampered the firefighting. The fire was finally brought under control by razing the Beadenkopf cottage at about 1:30 PM. The fire burned out of control for about an hour and forty-five minutes ultimately consuming 9 cottages, the camp meeting Tabernacle and the A. P. O. A. cottage. The *Sun* reported that half of the camp meeting place was destroyed with a loss of approximately $15,000.

The company records are incomplete between 1908 and late in 1912 and the first item of business recorded in the minutes for the year 1912 shows that a new piece of equipment was being considered. In October of 1912 it was decided to secure a hand drawn chemical apparatus from W. H. Whiting Company on approval for thirty days. The apparatus was delivered and demonstrated at an oyster supper and bazaar held on November 8 and 9 of 1912 at Redmen's Hall. The Redmen of Glyndon had offered their hall to the fire company for fund raising affairs on a number of occasions and would continue to do so in the years to come. Other community organizations such as the Ladies of Glyndon, Emory Grove and Glyndon Park also assisted the Fire Company in raising the funds essential to its continued operation by allowing the department the use of their facilities and equipment.

At the December 26, 1912 meeting of the company Mr. Wheeler, Chairman of the apparatus committee, reported that the apparatus had performed as specified and recommended that the company purchase it. The recommendation was accepted by the membership and the equipment purchased for the sum of $275.00. It is quite obvious that the purchase of new fire apparatus was considerably simpler when compared to the present, and cheaper too.

An airproof box was later constructed at the engine house to house the apparatus. Chemical Engines operated by mixing acid, usually sulphuric acid, with soda mixed with water in a pressure tank to generate carbon dioxide gas. The carbon dioxide gas then expelled the water from the pressure tank and on to the fire much as soda-acid fire extinguishers did in more recent times before their use was discontinued. The acid was kept separate from the soda-water mixture and added to the mixture at the fire scene. These chemicals made up the "charge" for the engine. The acid had to be protected from absorbing moisture from the air and loosing its potency hence the "airproof box." Chemical engines would be the mainstay of the fire service for some time to come and the Glyndon Company would own a number of them over the years. Soda and acid "charges" for the new chemical engine were purchased from E. G. Wheeler whose store was on Railroad Avenue. The store later owned by the Reter family and operated for many years as Reter's Store. The building currently houses the Glyndon General Store.

At the April 10, 1913, meeting a "committee was appointed to provide plans for the construction of a hall above the company's hall." The members of the committee are not identified in the minutes of that meeting. The hall committee reported at the June 25, 1913 meeting that, "nothing had been done to date." There is no further mention of this project in the company records and it was never carried out.

At the September 18, 1913 meeting "the subject of the purchasing new equipment was discussed and a motion made that each member of the committee appointed," the minutes do not provide their names; "obtain bids etc. on second hand automobiles, the chassis of which is to be used for the automobile fire truck." The resulting piece of apparatus, a White fire truck mounted on a Maxwell chassis, was the first motorized equipment purchased by the Glyndon Volunteer Fire Company. The Stansfield Brothers installed the White fire truck on the Maxwell chassis at a cost of $200.00, $75.00 in cas and $125.00 in notes payable within 4 months. Delivery of the apparatus was

C. Howard Whittle standing at the well and trough shortly after its completion. Current railroad station is seen in the background. (Courtesy BCPL)

taken in March of 1914. There are no surviving photographs of this apparatus.

At the same time that the new Maxwell apparatus was purchased, an offer was received from a Mr. Hack to donate a Panhart automobile, the chassis of which is to be used in "rigging up our Hook and Ladder truck." A motion was made to accept Mr. Hack's offer and a letter was sent to that effect. At the February 11, 1915 meeting it was agreed to ask Stansfield Brothers for a report "as to whether the Panhart chassis will be suitable for the Hook and Ladder truck." The minutes do not indicate what Stansfield Brothers reported but after considerable work and discussion, it was decided that the Panhart chassis would not be suitable and the idea was abandoned. The horses were not put out of work at this time but their days were numbered.

In June of 1914, a committee was appointed to see to certain repairs and improvements to the engine house, including such modern conveniences as electric lights. The company also decided to set the dues of the company at $.25 to defray the expense incurred in connection with social activities.

It is noted in the minutes of November 5, 1914, that the company elected a janitor to be paid a salary of $8.00 per month. The first member elected to the position of paid Janitor was Mr. Scott Bishop. The janitor was paid this sum until the company moved into the present building in 1956.

The year 1913 saw the formation of the Reisterstown Volunteer Fire Company. The Glyndon Company duly recognized this important event and entertained the new company on November 12, 1914.

The company entered the area of competitive sports in May of 1915, by fielding a baseball team. The team's first Manager was Mr. B. Sisk, assisted by Mr. H. Penn. The minutes indicate that the first game was played against the Boring Volunteer Fire Company team but fail to tell who won the game. The same month saw a motion to limit the speed of motor trucks to 35 mph for reasons of safety.

Sorrow came to the midst of the company in October of 1914 with the death of one of its most respected members, Mr. T. Reese Arnold. The company paid its final tribute in a resolution marking the great loss felt by the company on the death of one of its original members and officers. Mr. Arnold was Treasurer of the company at the time of his death, an office he had held since the organization of the company in 1904. The following epitaph, quoted from the resolution seems to sum the emotion that was felt at that time:

"God calleth a man who did noble work,
In his life, without looking for gain,
Whose smile always brightened and cheered up the heart,
And made sunshine midst sorrow and rain.
We firemen will miss him, whose laugh we all knew,
May his soul rest in peace at God's will,
We mourn his great loss, and his family console
There's no one that place can fill."

J. Henry Albrecht – G.V.F.D

Feeling the need of a water supply in the community, a committee was appointed on October 14, 1915, to contact the Western Maryland Railroad and ask permission to install a well, pump and concrete watering trough on their property opposite Redmen's Hall and C. G. Wheeler's store. The committee consisting of Messrs. G. Howard Whittle, Edwin R. Stringer and G. Edgar Penn, contacted the Railroad and the company was given a lease on the desired piece of property. To help pay for the well the company organized and produced a minstrel show on March 4, 1916. The show was so good that the company was requested to put it on at various other places in Baltimore and Carroll Counties. Being unable to keep members of the minstrel company together, they were not able to accept these engagements.

The well was dug in June of 1916.The trough and cover were designed by the Ladies of Glyndon. The work was completed in November of 1916 and the completion duly noted by the following resolution:

"Whereas there has been for years the necessity for a well and pump in the vicinity of Glyndon station, and whereas the Glyndon Volunteer Fire Company realizing such a necessity undertook to have a well drilled and pump installed.

And, whereas, an artesian well with a bountiful supply of good, pure water has been completed."

"And whereas, it was through the untiring efforts of the President of the fire company that said well was pushed to completion. Therefore, be it resolved that the Glyndon Volunteer Fire Company does hereby extend its most sincere thanks to Mr. C. Howard Whittle, its President, for the successful manner in which he handled this proposition. And be it further resolved that a copy of these resolutions be spread upon the minutes of the company and a copy therefore sent to its President."

The fire department still leases the property, and the well and trough are still to be seen on Railroad Avenue opposite The Glyndon General Store (then Wheelers store). Until recently the building housed Reter's Store. Community organizations have assisted the department in maintaining the structure over the years

Fire alarms at the time were received from the telephone exchange in Reisterstown. A committee was appointed in December of 1915 to contact the Telephone Company and see that the company was notified promptly in the event of a fire in their area. The company further decided to investigate the feasibility of installing "some kind of fire alarm system."

On July 5, 1916, the standing committee reported that a Federal motor truck had been ordered to be attached to the present Hook and Ladder and that the new equipment was to be installed as soon as possible. They also went on to explain that the price to be paid for

Contemporary Photo of the well and trough. (GVFD Photo)

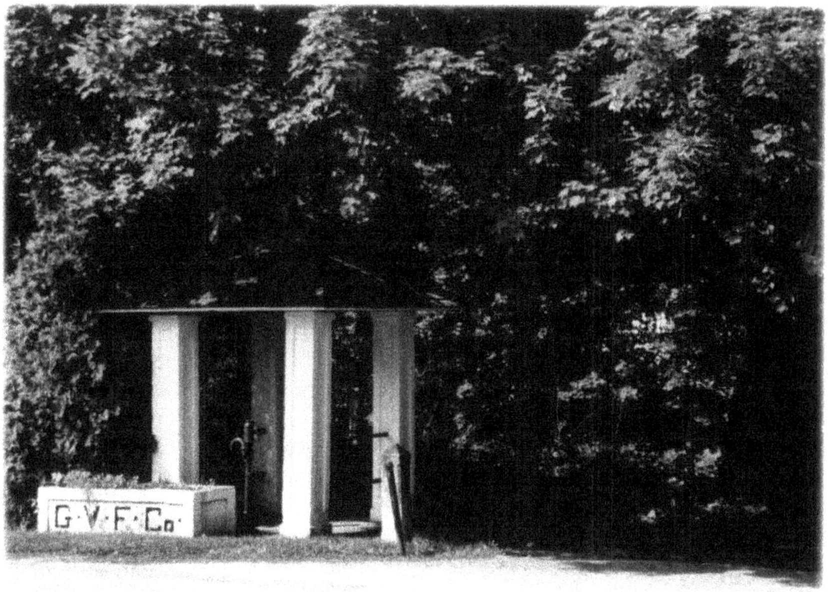

the chassis was $1,900.00. One hundred dollars to be paid when contract was signed, nine hundred dollars on delivery and nine hundred dollars covered by notes to mature in one year at 6 percent. Specifications for the truck were a 30hp motor, a 1-1/2 ton capacity with 1/2 ton overhead, equipped with two search-lights, a speedometer, a Bosch magneto, Swinehart cellular tires, 3-1/2 inch front and 6 inch rear. The truck was to be delivered F.O.B. Glyndon. Photographs of the Federal truck rigged to the Hook and Ladder show that it was also equipped with a two tank chemical system making it a formidable piece of fire fighting equipment for that time. It is believed that the motorized Hook and Ladder truck, as reported in the minutes of the company, was the first piece of apparatus of its kind in the State.

The matter of raising money has always been an important one to the company. Since the organization of the company, numerous fund raising activities have been held. The minutes of the company show that regular lawn fetes, bazaars, carnivals and suppers had been held over the years. The first fund raising activities were held on the lawn in Glyndon Park and later in front of the State Road Garage. More recently, Glyndon held an annual carnival at the Reisterstown Firemen's Grove. The Carnivals were discontinued in the 1960s. The Grove has since been sold by the Reisterstown Volunteer Fire Company and commercially developed.

1916 Federal Hook & Ladder in front of home in Emory Grove. Members (L to R) C. Howard Whittle, Enoch Channey, Gray Baublitz, William Roylston, Edward Wheeler, J. Edward Hewes, Charles Sentz, John Roylston, John Peffer, Edgar Penn and Granville Baublitz. Seen in the window on the left - Mrs. Peffer. (GVFD Archives)

These early events were truly community affairs with local organizations and residents assisting in their success. It is recorded that the Glyndon Park Group had charge of the candy table at one of the lawn fetes. The Women's Group offered to arrange a cake sale at the same affair. The Daughter's of America took charge of the lemonade stand. At an earlier affair, Mr. Lester Wheeler donated a $2.50 gold piece, which was raffled off at 5 cents a chance.

The Federal truck was completed in September of 1916, and an evening of entertainment was scheduled for October 5, 1916, to show the new apparatus to the community. Music was arranged for and refreshments served.

1916 Federal Apparatus and members. (L to R) on Truck: Walter Snyder, J. Edward Bollinger, John Roylston, Edward Wilson, Grafton C. Wheeler, Charles W. Fishpaw, Charles E Sentz. On the ground: C. Howard Whittle and William Roylston. (GVFD Archives)

After the Hook and Ladder was taken out of service, the Federal truck was built up as a fire engine, with the addition of a body built by Mr. Hobb of Owings Mills. The apparatus was maintained in service until the 1930s when it was sold to Mr. Robert Wirtz.

At the October 12, 1916 meeting, Mr. N. Smith moved that a committee be appointed to place an order for a bell. A committee composed of Geo. Penn, Fred Thome and Enoch Channey was appointed and charged with ordering a bell. They completed their work in short order and the bell was delivered in November of 1916 and served as the public fire alarm until the purchase of the siren in 1928. In addition to the public alarm, an electric bell arrangement in the homes of key members was also installed. During the day, alarms were received by Mr. E. G. Wheeler at his store on Railroad Avenue. In the evening, alarms were received by Mr. Edward Bollinger at his home. Mr. Bollinger called the Captain and sounded the electric bell summoning other members to respond. On arrival at the engine house the public alarm was sounded.

Mr. Ed Hewes tells us that his home was not included in the alarm system, but on hearing the bell in a nearby home his dog would bark and alert him to the alarm.

1916 Federal Apparatus and members in front of the Glyndon Railroad Station. Members (L to R): Bill Roylston, C. Howard Whittle, Ridgley Pierce, Abram L. Geist, Walter S. Snyder, J. Edward Bollinger. (GVFD Archives)

Since the Reisterstown Volunteer Fire Company also used a bell as a public alarm, a code of three taps was sounded on the Glyndon bell to summon the members so there would be no confusion as to which alarm bell was being sounded. The public alarm bell was loaned to the Gill's Church on a permanent basis when the company moved to its new building in 1956. The bell has since been returned and is displayed in front of the current station.

The only known fatal fire in the Glyndon fire alarm territory occurred in June of 1917 when Mr. Geo. P. Brown was burned to death in his

1916 Federal apparatus training at the old Glyndon Post Office and Wheeler's Store. At the truck - Howard Whittle. On the roof - Edgar Penn. On the pump - Edward Bollinger (L) and Ridgely Pierce. (GVFD Archives)

home in Woodensburg. Messrs. Ed Hewes and Norman Fritz tell us that the fire was hot and smoky and not having gas masks at that time the rescue efforts were severely hampered. Mr. Brown's body was later recovered from the basement of the building by the firemen. A letter was received from Ms. Stella E. Brown and read at the July 16, 1917 meeting thanking the company for their "assistance in trying to locate the body of her father who burned up in the recent fire."

The December 17, 1917 meeting of the company saw a change in the titles of the officers. The Chief Foreman's title was changed to Captain and the Assistant Foreman changed to Lieutenant

During World War I, the members of the various volunteer fire companies volunteered to serve as home guards. The engine house was manned during the evenings and throughout the night. It was even suggested that the installation of a gun rack on the truck might be a good idea. The gun rack matter was dropped, probably to the good of all concerned, fire department rivalries being as they were in those days.

The years between 1917 and 1922 were quickly consumed in the routine business of the fire company, the most significant item of which was, as you might expect, fund raising.

In February of 1922 the company, feeling the need of a more modern piece of fire equipment, purchased a Pierce Arrow touring car. A water pump, powered by the vehicle's engine, was added to this chassis by a machine company in Baltimore. The pump was to pump "30 gallons per minute through a standard nozzle at normal rate of speed" The pump proved to be unsatisfactory in that it would not meet the specifications. The motor in the truck was "burned out" trying to pump the apparatus to its capacity. The motor was replaced with one from a Pierce Arrow hearse purchased in Baltimore.

1922 Pierce Arrow Chemical Engine. (GVFD Archives)

A prolonged discussion with the company installing the pump ensued, including several tests of the pump with a Mr. Hollingsworth, a representative of the company that installed the pump, finally resulting with the fire company being sued for the cost of the pump. The suit was subsequently dismissed. With the failure of the pump, the company decided to have the chassis equipped with a four tank chemical apparatus manufactured by the Fomite-Childs Company.

The chemical equipment was designed by Mr. Ed Hewes of the Glyndon Volunteer Fire Company. The completed truck was delivered in November of 1923 and demonstrated at the Thanksgiving Day supper. The total cost of the truck, after modification, was about $2,800.00. This equipment was kept in service until 1937 when it was replaced by a new Ford engine.

With the acquisition of the 1922 Pierce Arrow the fire company had two modern fire trucks, the other being the 1916 Federal. Both were equipped with chemically activated water tanks, the standard of the time. As with the 1912 hand drawn chemical engine, these motorized chemical engines required the mixing of the soda and acid to generate carbon dioxide gas to provide the pressure for the water stream. At that time engine driven water pumps were not common as equipment on fire apparatus.

The New Year of 1924 was ushered in with a bang with a motion duly made and seconded that the trucks be washed. Helmets and goggles were ordered and purchased for the drivers, with a fine of $1.00 for removing them from the engine house except in case of responding to a fire alarm. The bell used as a public alarm was supplemented by a Klaxon horn. This device was later replaced by a six volt siren because the horn was not loud enough. Nineteen twenty-seven saw the alarm committee considering the purchase and installation of a large electric siren. This project was not to reach fruition until the fall of 1928.

Nineteen twenty-eight was an important year in the growth of the company. Mrs. C. B. Arnold was elected as a member. This is the first record of a woman member. Later records show several women members including Mrs. C. F. Eckhardt, Mrs. J. E. Bollinger, Mrs. R. C. McKee, Mrs. A. A. Dyer and Mrs. Elizabeth Hammond. Mrs. Mary Lauterbach was the last woman member of the company until 1974 and was actively engaged in the work of the company for over twenty-five years.

The failure of the pump installed on the Pierce Arrow to meet the specifications delayed the introduction of a pumping fire engine by the company until 1928. At the February 13, 1928 meeting a committee consisting of Capt. Snyder, John O. Cockey, E. Channey and Carlton Chilcoat, was appointed to purchase a new engine. A new American LaFrance truck equipped with a modern water pump was delivered to the company in June of 1928 at a cost of $10,353.00. This equipment was maintained in service until replaced by a new Mack truck in 1947 at which time it was sold to the Middle River Volunteer Fire Company.

A piece of property and a building were purchased from Rodger and Clarence Stansfield for the sum of $1,200.00. The building was rented for a number of years and finally sold to the State Roads Commission.

1928 American LaFrance engine. Seen at Middle River VFD. (GVFD Archives)

1922 Pierce Arrow Chemical Engine at the Great Reisterstown Fire. (GVFD Archives)

The new siren was ordered in June of 1928. It was a five horsepower double ended siren and cost $490.00. Both Federal and Sterling models were considered and the final order was placed with the Sterling Siren Fire Alarm Company. The siren was installed in September of 1928.

The C&P Telephone Company was contracted to supply a direct telephone line to the Glyndon fire station to blow the siren when ever an alarm was received by the C&P operator in Reisterstown. Later, when the county wide radio system was established, the siren was blown by radio from a central dispatch in the Towson Fire Station.

This siren was moved to the new building in 1956 and remained in service until 1969 when it was replaced with a more modern siren. The siren continues to be blown by radio but the dispatch of all county emergency services is now handled by the 911 Center in Towson, Maryland. The siren continues to be the principle public alarm system for the Glyndon Volunteer Fire Department.

On February 11, 1928, the town of Reisterstown suffered a disastrous fire to the Main Street business district. The *Baltimore News* reported that five buildings were destroyed and that the entire business district was threatened. All the buildings involved were two story business structures with apartments occupying the second floor. A number of families were turned out of their apartments in freezing weather by this early morning fire. The *Baltimore News* went on to report that two firemen were overcome by smoke. Water was in short supply and was pumped from a pond two miles from the town.

Sixteen fire companies including the Glyndon Volunteer Fire Company responded to the fire to assist the Reisterstown Volunteer Fire Company. "Philip G. Priester, chief of the Baltimore County Fire Department, directed the operations. Five thousand gallons of chemicals were used according to Chief Priester." The Reisterstown Volunteer Fire Company reported in their 50th anniversary book that the damage resulting from this fire amounted to $250,000.

Glyndon Methodist Church prior to the 1929 fire. (Courtesy BCPL)

A long-standing custom of the fire company was established in 1929. At this time a "poor box" was started to which each member made a small contribution each week to pay for periodic feeds after the meetings. The first collection, taken at the September 30, 1929, meeting amounted to $2.16. The "poor box" has been replaced by a 50-50 raffle held at the department's weekly meetings.

Conflagration came to Glyndon on December 8, 1929, when the Glyndon Methodist Church was destroyed by fire. The fire, members who were there recall, was one of the hottest in the history of the company. The fire completely consumed the church, the parsonage, the men's bible class building and the home of Mr. Arnold. The fire threatened to spread to other buildings but was contained through the efforts of mutual aid fire companies from Reisterstown, Owings Mills, Arcadia, Boring and Westminster. The career engine from Pikesville also responded.

Ruins of Arnold home destroyed by 1929 church fire. (GVFD Archives)

The blaze started in the Sunday school classroom and, fanned by a strong wind, extended to the church and parsonage. The fire then leaped about 40 feet to the Arnold home. Mr. Arnold was a director of the Glyndon Bank and a member of the Glyndon Fire Company. He also served as President of the Baltimore County Volunteer Firemen's Association. Mrs. T. Rowe Price reported the fire to the Glyndon Fire Company. The Pastor, Daniel W. Justice and his family were forced from the parsonage. Mr. Arnold carried his mother from the house and joined his neighbors in saving the furniture from the parsonage and his home. Despite the high winds, the responding fire companies were able to stop the spread of the fire and save the home of Lester Wheeler. The loss due to the fire was estimated to be at least $60,000.

Founded in 1924, The Men's Bible Class, officially known as the Glyndon Community Men's Bible Class, started with six members but grew quickly to the point where it was decided to build a separate building. The original building was begun in 1927 and destroyed shortly after its completion by the 1929 church fire. Following the fire the Bible Class continued to meet at sites throughout Reisterstown,

In July of 1930, the men's bible class building was rebuilt and church services were held there. The new building included a kitchen and a theatrical stage as well as meeting space for the Bible Class. The building has been used by a number of community organizations, over the years, presenting plays and using the facility for special meetings. The building was moved to its present location in 1957 to make room for the expansion of the church. The organization continued to grow under the leadership of George Seabold and is an important community organization today. In the 1980s a Ladies Auxiliary was formed and the class began to accept women as members and became the Glyndon Community Bible Class.

Ruins of the Glyndon Methodist Church after 1929 fire. (GVFD Archives)

The Glyndon Community Men's Bible Class has been closely aligned with the Glyndon Volunteer Fire Department. Over the years, members of the fire department have been both members and leaders of the Men's Bible Class. In the 1960s the number of fire department members attending the Sunday morning class was so large that a pumper was parked next to the Bible Class building so it

Community Men's Bible Class building rebuilt after 1929 Glyndon Methodist Church fire. (GVFD Photo)

could respond quickly in case an alarm was received during the class.

The cornerstone of the new church building was laid in October of 1930 and the building was completed in 1931. This structure is located on the site of the old church on Butler Road.

The depression years and the late thirties saw the company maintain the status quo despite the bad times that most people experienced during these years. In 1937, the company again voted to modernize its apparatus and purchased a 1937 Ford truck. The chassis was purchased from Beall Motors at a cost of $588.00. The truck was built up by the members of the company and was equipped with a midship rotary gear pump, the standard of the time, and a water tank. The truck was later modified to add a ladder that was affixed to the truck and operated in a manner similar to a ladder truck. The truck was modified again to serve as a field fire piece and a Gorman-Rupt portable pump was added in October of 1949. This equipment was in service with the company until replaced in 1961 by a 1951 Dodge power wagon. At that time the Ford truck was sold to F. L. Anderson Company for $500.00.

December 7, 1941, brought the nation to a state of war and the Glyndon Volunteer Fire Department plunged into the important work of active civil defense. The members, who were left at home, after many left to serve in the armed forces, served as air raid wardens, messengers and in other capacities in the civil defense effort. The minutes of December 8, 1941 make no mention of the tragic and history making events of the previous day. However the department mobilized quickly and on December 15, 1941 forty-two members of the department and community residents met to mobilize for Civil Defense. The minutes of that meeting chronicle an extensive discussion of such matters as the use of hand grenades and flame throwers and fighting incendiary fires. A detailed discussion of various chemical agents the department might face was also conducted along with instructions on identifying the various types of ordinance the department might encounter. The minutes of January 26, 1941 lists these 14 members who were trained to serve as Air Raid Wardens: Daniel Talbert, Elam Geist, George Turnbaugh, William Pearson, Buck Lealy, Louis Woodward, James E. Carter, James Molesworth, Pierce Harris, Carroll Brown, Edwin Molesworth, Sam Wesley, Walter Harris and Yeatts Wilson. The Glyndon Volunteer Fire Department and the residents of Glyndon, were determined to be prepared to protect the community against any eventuality.

Glyndon Methodist Church building rebuilt after 1929 fire. (GVFD Photo)

Gasoline was rationed and the department was allotted twenty gallons a

1937 Ford Pumper. (GVFD Photo)

month with the ration book being kept by Mr. Walter Harris. A priority was obtained to purchase a fog nozzle that was a new innovation in fire fighting and considered essential for fighting incendiary bomb fires. The department regularly purchased war bonds in large amounts and supported its members overseas by sending cigarettes.

With the war years past, the department placed an order for a 1947 Mack fire truck. A committee consisting of Walter Harris, Edwin Molesworth, Sr. and Carlton Chilcoat supervised the preparation of the specifications for the new apparatus. The truck was equipped with equipment and hose removed from the American LaFrance and so equipped was one of the most modern fire trucks in the county. This truck was in first line service with the company until June of 1966.

As early as 1948, the company felt that the existing engine house on Railroad Avenue was not adequate. Modern fire apparatus was larger than the equipment for which the building was originally constructed and meeting room facilities were inadequate. The first step toward the new building was taken in October of 1948 when Messrs. C. Chilcoat and J. E. Warner, Sr., were appointed as a committee to see Wade Emmett in regard to purchasing a piece of ground on Butler Road for a new engine house. Between 1948 and 1952 other locations were considered and investigated including a parcel at the corner of Glyndon Avenue. The Butler Road site was finally selected and purchased subject to zoning in November of 1952 for $5,000.00.

A building committee consisting of George Arnold, John O. Cockey, Paul Boller, Carlton Chilcoat and James Warner, Jr.,

1947 Mack Pumper. (GVFD Photo)

Glyndon Fire Company Eyes New Location On Butler Rd.

For

George W. Arnold of Glyndon said this week:

"The proposed new Glyndon fire house would be located on the Butler road opposite the Glyndon Bank, which is the best location available. The lot has ample room for a large building and plenty of parking space off the highway.

"The Glyndon Fire Company has outgrown its present quarters. The present building and ramp cover all the ground the fire company owns, which makes it impossible to have either a toilet or a shower, since there is no room for a septic tank.

"The meeting room is too small. In fact when the Baltimore County Volunteer Firemen's Association comes to Glyndon for a meeting outside quarters have to be provided. This is not satisfactory. Anticipating a new building, the ladies wish to form an auxiliary, which is an important adjunct to any fire company.

"The Glyndon Volunteer Fire Company was organized in 1904 and has given valuable services to the community. For several years the company has been saving funds, hoping to be in a position to arrange for a more desirable location.

"These men work without pay and are even willing to go out and fight a fire for someone trying to obstruct their progress, as well as for others.

"All the Glyndon Fire Company is asking is that the good citizens of our community get behind this project and help it to fulfillment."

Against

About 80% of residents of the Butler road, Glyndon signed a petition opposing construction of a new Glyndon fire house at the location proposed by the Glyndon Volunteer Fire Company.

This petition was presented at a hearing before Augustine J. Muller, county Zoning Commissioner, on Tuesday, February 3, when a hearing was held on the subject of erecting a new Glyndon fire house on Butler road. No zoning is required, but the fire company would have to obtain a building permit, which is issued through the county Zoning and Buildings Department.

Opponents of the proposed location of a new Glyndon fire house said that Butler road is a quiet, residential area and that location of a fire engine house there is not appropriate and would depreciate property values in the neighborhood.

The hearing on Feb. 3 was premature, which was pointed out by Mr. Muller when it developed that the Glyndon Volunteer Fire Company has no plans or specifications ready for the proposed new building. Mr. Muller said that plans must be submitted before any further moves can be made in the situation.

Opponents of the new fire house location pointed out that they have been supporters of the Glyndon Volunteer Fire Company and feel that the company should seriously reconsider its present plans before incurring the risk of offending a considerable number of Glyndon property owners.

Pro – Con, the community expresses their views on the proposed new firehouse. (BCPL files. Newspaper unknown)

was appointed on June 15, 1953. This committee solicited ideas on what should be included in the new building from the members and prepared the preliminary plans for submittal to the architect.

Zoning approval had been given in February of 1953, but there was considerable disagreement within the Glyndon community as to the suitability of the location selected for the new station. Due to appeals to the zoning decision, a building permit was not issued until November of 1953.

Preliminary plans were drawn by the firm of W. T. Mullen, Architects, and were approved by the department in May of 1954. Bids were solicited in January of 1955 and construction was begun shortly thereafter. The company took occupancy of the building in February of 1956. The new building was completed at a cost of $74,000.

The new facility provided larger quarters for equipment providing for the housing of the additional apparatus needed to meet the needs of a growing Glyndon community. A community hall and kitchen were included in the building providing a place for the department and the community to hold affairs. The hall is made available to the community at a nominal rental for dances and the like.

The old building was sold in December of 1956 to Robert Albright for $3,700.00. It was later owned by Russ Lessner, a member of the department, who operated an automobile repair garage in the building. Later, North West Radiator co-operated in the building. The present occupant is Spedo UK Ltd.

At the same time that the building was being built another important step was taken to provide better fire protection to the community and the county as a whole. Mobile radio sets were installed in the apparatus to provide rapid communication with the trucks. Using these new radios any company could quickly summon help to a fire or be advised to proceed to other alarms while still on the road. Previously when a company required assistance at a fire, it was necessary to summon help by means of a nearby telephone. In January of 1954, a base station radio set was installed in the engine house and shortly thereafter control of the siren was given over to radio control from a Central Alarm Headquarters in Towson. The telephone line was subsequently discontinued and an era came to an end.

The New Glyndon Firehouse. (GVFD Archives)

In November of 1958, the department voted to purchase a Cab Forward, Model C 85 Mack pumper at a cost of $26,800.00. This decision was the culmination of many months of work by the truck committee consisting of Raymond Warner, James W. Beck, Edwin Molesworth, Jr. and James E. Warner, Jr.

In the months following the appointment of the committee, many different manufacturers of apparatus were investigated and their equipment tried by the committee. The decision to purchase the Mack pumper placed the most modern piece of fire apparatus in the county at the disposal of the Glyndon community. An important feature of the truck was the 800 Gallon water tank with which it was equipped. This large water supply made it possible to make a fast initial attack even on a large fire without the need for fire hydrants that are in short supply in a large portion of the Glyndon Volunteer Fire Department's first alarm area. A portable electric power generator was also fitted to the truck to provide lights at fires and when power outages occurred. This generator also allowed the company to maintain radio communication during a power outage caused by a storm or other emergency. The new equipment was delivered in May of 1959.

1959 Mack model C85 Pumper. (Photo by Joel Woods)

While responding to an alarm of fire on Park Heights Avenue, on December 26, 1959, this equipment fell through a bridge on a private lane leading to the fire scene. The weight of the truck was 27,400 pounds. Fortunately, the wooden bridge was supported by steel beams and the truck came to rest on the beams with little damage to the equipment and no injuries. Once the fire was extinguished, the problem of extricating the truck was tackled. With the assistance of Mr. Ross Yox, the truck was jacked up and towed back to the main road.

Work on another piece of new equipment was begun in September of 1960, when a 1951 Dodge Power Wagon Navy weapons carrier was purchased from the Government for $125.00. This vehicle was purchased with the idea that it would make a fine piece of apparatus for field fires.

1951 Dodge Power Wagon Brush Unit. (GVFD Archives)

A committee consisting of James Warner, Jr., Leroy Wolfgang and Casey Caples prepared a design for the truck and presented it to the department in January of 1961. The engine was equipped with a Panama pump and tank and a body built to the company's specifications and drawings by the F. L. Anderson Company of Baltimore.

The new piece was put in service April 12, 1961. A winch was added to the apparatus in January of 1962. The 1937 Ford truck was sold to the F. L. Anderson Company for $500.00. This truck had only 14,586 miles on it when it was sold after twenty-four years of service.

The total cost of the Dodge Power Wagon when completed was $1,996.18. This piece of apparatus was in service until March of 1972 when it was replaced with an International Scout.

In January of 1964, a committee consisting of President C. Leroy Wolfgang, J. Peter Brach, Jr., Cornelius E. Cole, James E. Warner, Jr., Richard W. Stem, Sr., Richard Merriken and Calvin Reter was appointed to organize a program of events to celebrate the 60th anniversary of the department's founding. Under the direction of this committee and with the assistance of the entire membership, a year-long program of events was prepared. The 60th anniversary celebration was kicked off at the annual banquet in March of 1964 where the department was presented with resolutions from both the House and Senate of the Maryland legislature honoring their 60th birthday. The department distributed small first aid kits to all the residents of the community as a remembrance of the anniversary year.

In August of 1964, a gala carnival was held with a large parade and a special 60th anniversary exhibit. It was one of the best ever. The celebration was closed on March 6, 1965, again at the annual banquet with the community being presented with a commemorative book telling the story of the first 60 years of service by the Glyndon Volunteer Fire Department. The historical notes contained in the book served as a tribute to the community's support through those first 60 years, and a request for their continued support in the years to come.

With electricity being an absolutely necessity to providing emergency services to their community, and with the success provided by their portable generator, it was decided to look for a large stationary generator at the State Civil Defense surplus warehouse. In October of 1964, the department purchased a diesel generator capable of providing electric power to the firehouse as well as powering the siren during a power failure. An enclosure for the generator was built next to the station on the ground level. The generator was connected by C. E. Cole an electrical contractor and a member of the department. This generator, costing $100.00, served until June of 1970, when a larger 25 kw generator was purchased from the State Civil Defense warehouse at Jessup, Maryland, also at a cost of $100.00. The Grinnell Corporation generously picked the unit up at Jessup and using their boom truck, placed it in the emergency generator room located beside the station that housed the first generator. C. E. Cole connected the new generator

During these many years the department saw no need to lock the entrance door to the firehouse. This allowed the members to enter quickly when responding to an alarm of fire. However, with the changing times, a larger population, and more and more transient traffic through the town, it was found necessary to lock the door. A card key lock was installed on the entrance door in February of 1965. This system allowed rapid entrance to the station when required, using a coded card issued to each member. This system was later replaced with a push button combination lock that provided better control over who was authorized to enter the building. The door control system has since been updated to a sophisticated key tag system connected to the station computer.

The system controls the entry to a number outside doors to the building allowing members convenient entry.

In February of 1965, the department upgraded its communications system by replacing their aging 1954 era base station radio with a new unit at a cost of $530.00. The addition of the new base station radio significantly improved the reliability of the system and reduced maintenance requirements. Over the years both base station and mobile radios have been regularly updated to improve performance.

President C. L. Wolfgang appointed a committee in July 1965 to investigate the purchase of a new engine to replace the 1947 Mack pumper. The committee for this new project consisted of Chief James E. Warner, Jr., Calvin Reter, Jere Whiteside, Charles Gore, Vernon Merkel and Raymond Warner. The committee reported their findings to the department and recommended that the department purchase another Mack, a cab forward pumper with a diesel engine and 750 gpm waterous pump and a 750 gallon water tank at a cost of $30,368.00.

This engine was the same body style as the Mack pumper purchased in 1959 giving the department the distinction of having "twin pumpers." The company was given $3,368.00 in trade for the 1947 Mack, leaving a balance of $27,000.00 to the purchase price. The contract was signed on October 19, 1965 and delivery was made in May of 1966. The unit was placed in service June 26, 1966. The first emergency response was to assist the Reisterstown Volunteer Fire Company on a call for fluorescent light ballast on June 29, 1966.

The years 1966 and 1967 were dedicated to the routine business of the fire company with the most significant effort, as always, being fund raising to pay for the new apparatus.

The department, as has been reported, made significant contributions to the Civil Defense during the First and Second World Wars. In the late 1960s as the Cold War escalated and the threat of atomic attack became all too real, the department was again called upon to protect the Glyndon community. In the event of an atomic attack, Baltimore and Washington, DC were considered prime targets, the Glyndon Volunteer Fire Department would be the first line of community defense.

Beginning in 1967, members of the department were trained in basic atomic physics and in the use of a number of radiological measuring instruments. In the event of an attack, the department would make measurements of the amount of radioactive fall out and report to Civil Defense authorities. Glyndon was designated as a fixed monitoring station and assigned the call 6ETQ.

A 1968 report indicated that the level of protection provided against fallout by the firehouse was below

1966 Mack Pumper, the department's first Diesel powered apparatus. (Photo by Joel Woods)

the minimum required for use as a public shelter but was sufficient to protect the fire department personnel and operate the monitoring station. Supplies of water, food and other necessities were stored at the firehouse to supply the department's members in the event of an attack.

Regular drills were held from 1969 through 1974. With the end of the cold war the threat of atomic attack subsided and 6ETQ was deactivated and the instruments returned to the county.

Early 1968 brought tragic event in the department's history. On February 19, 1968 while on a fire call, one of our most respected members, Raymond Otto, suffered a heart attack and died on the fire grounds. This is the only "in the line of duty" death known to have occurred in the history of the department.

In April 1968, the department became aware that the Seabold property, a converted house containing two apartments, adjoining the department's property on the east side was for sale. Realizing that the department might need to expand in the future, an offer to buy the property was made. The department's offer was accepted and the purchase completed in late April of 1968 for $25,000.00. A decision was made to continue to rent the two apartments in the building to help pay the mortgage.

The year of 1969 passed with the continued effort to raise funds to reduce the department debt.

In July of 1970, a partial sprinkler system was installed in the firehouse. The system provides fire protection to the equipment room and if activated blows the station siren alerting the members of the department to the emergency. The system was made possible through the generosity of the following businesses:

- AUTOMATIC SPRINKLER CORPORATION OF AMERICA
- C. E. COLE, ELECTRICAL CONTRACTOR
- GRINNELL COMPANY, INC.
- INGLESIDE PLUMBING & HEATING COMPANY, INC.
- A. C. MacDONALD COMPANY, INC.

The Seabold property, purchased by the department in 1968 as a rental property and for future expansion. (GVFD Photo)

These are men and companies dedicated to the preservation of life and property through fire protection.

In February of 1971, the department purchased two Meushaw hydrant valves from F. L. Anderson Co. at a cost of $375.00 each. The addition of these appliances allowed engine 401 and engine 403 to lay hose from a hydrant and receive water from the hydrant immediately without waiting for a second pumper to arrive, connect to the hydrant and pump the supply line to the attack pumper at the fire scene. The second arriving pumper, instead, was able to connect to the hydrant and "pump the supply line" with out interrupting the water supply to the fire grounds. The appliance markedly improved the efficiency of the department in "getting water on the fire."

Also, in February 1971, President E. R. Brown, Sr., appointed a committee to replace Brush Unit 402, the government surplus Dodge Power Wagon, placed in service April 12, 1961. The committee consisted of Jere Whiteside, C. E. Cole, R. Warner, J. Warner, Jr. and E. R. Brown, Sr. The committee recommended, and the department approved, the purchase an International Scout II from C. R. Lynch Co. of Reisterstown. Members of the department built up the brush unit. The Scout was delivered to the department on March 3, 1972 with all the mechanical work finished, the radio installed and the paint and lettering completed. The 1972 International Scout II, "new Brush Unit 402," was placed in service on April 20, 1972 at a cost of $5,877.99. The new brush unit was funded through a generous donation from the ladies auxiliary. A plaque recognizing the generous contribution of the Ladies Auxiliary was affixed to the new apparatus.

The Dodge Power Wagon was sold to the Oren Co. of Roanoke, Va. for $900.00.

The International brush truck remained in first line service until 1995. At that time, with the number of field and wood fires declining as the rural areas of the district were developed, the department decided to offer the unit for sale. In August of 1995 bids were solicited and Michael Warner, a member of the department, was the successful bidder with a bid of $300.

A significant improvement in firefighter safety was made in April of 1971 when the Baltimore County Volunteer Firemen's Association directed that all volunteer companies remove their "All Service Masks" from service. The All Service Mask only filtered the smoke and combustion products from the air and required that the oxygen level in the fire area be high enough to sustain life. The modern, man made, materials, particularly plastics, found in most occupancies often depleted the oxygen level below acceptable levels and generated combustion products that the All Service mask was not designed to filter. This placed a firefighter entering a burning building at significant risk of injury or death.

Only self-contained type masks, those that did not require a breathable atmosphere, such as the Chemox oxygen generating mask and Self Contained Breathing Apparatus (SCBA) that use compressed air in tanks were approved for use by Baltimore County volunteer departments. The Glyndon Volunteer

1972 International Brush unit donated by the Ladies Auxiliary. (Photo by Joel Woods)

Fire Department purchased 3 SurviveAir SCBA masks each for engine 401 and engine 403 and retained the 2 Chemox masks already carried on each engine. The Chemox masks have since been removed from service and replaced with additional SCBA.

In response to the increasing number of emergency calls being dispatched, Baltimore County updated its fire department communications system by expanding the radio system to four channels. The addition of two channels to the system provided dedicated channels for fire ground operations. As a result the Glyndon Volunteer Fire Department replaced all of the two channel radios in their equipment with new four channel radios in September of 1971.

In October of 1971, the department purchased their first 3" hose. Until this time each engine was equipped with 1200' of 2-1/2" hose. The first order was for 750 feet of hose. This was loaded in a split load of 600 feet of 3" hose and 600 feet of 2-1/2" hose on engine 401. The addition of 3" hose to the apparatus allowed larger volumes of water to be pumped through the same length of hose significantly improving firefighting efficiency. A short time later the remaining 2-1/2" hose in service on our engines was retired and replaced with 3" hose.

Things were relatively quiet during 1972 and 1973 while the department took another break to concentrate on raising money to sustain the department.

January of 1974 brought sewage to the town of Glyndon and the department's buildings were immediately connected. The department added recessed lighting to their hall, invested in a color TV set to replace the worn out black and white model, and applied for and received a bulk-mailing permit which considerably reduced the cost of our mail solicitation.

In October of 1974, with the number of alarms rapidly increasing, the department found itself continually short of manpower during the normal workday. To serve their community better, the company accepted as members and trained seven female firefighters to help man the equipment. These seven female firefighters were Maxine D. Warner, Rosemary Stem, Maxine E. Warner, Carol Beimschla, Mary Merriken, Donna Warner and Jill Warner. All passed the University of Maryland Basic Firefighter's Course. These intrepid women were a history making addition to the department. Although not the first women members of the department, there were others in the early days of the department's history, they were the first to be formally trained as firefighters and to respond to alarms. Of course in the beginning these were not the "best dressed" women in town at the fire scene. Until the department was able to purchase firefighting gear specifically designed to fit these new firefighters they used the available gear that was not always a "good fit."

Two of the department's female firefighters later served as fire suppression officers. In 1989 Dorothy Schultz served as a Lieutenant and was the first female line officer. Kathy Wolfenden served as a Lieutenant in 1992.

In late 1974 another step was taken to increase the manpower available to respond to alarms. The department offered members first option on renting the company's apartments next door. At least one active firefighting member has occupied an apartment since the program was established.

The time required to assemble a crew and respond to an alarm is critical to the successful outcome of any emergency incident. The members of the department began to purchase and use monitor radios so they could receive an alarm at the same time the station was alerted and did not have to depend on the siren. This shortened the time required to get to the station. An eclectic mix of military surplus tank radios and commercially manufactured monitor radios was assembled over the years by the members of the department at their own expense.

Beginning in January of 1975, many members purchased tone alert radios manufactured by the Motorola Company to replace their conventional radios at a cost of $226.00 each. The tone alert radios sounded an audible alarm when the Glyndon Volunteer Fire Department siren was toned to blow by the county fire dispatcher. The new radios modernized the department's alert system cutting minutes off the response time and assuring larger crews during night time hours.

Some of the history of the Glyndon Volunteer Fire Department has been preserved in an old bell mounted on a stand in the meeting room. This bell was first used on the 1928 American LaFrance when responding to an emergency. When the American LaFrance was sold, the bell was moved to the then new 1947 Mack Pumper. It was subsequently removed from the unit when the 1947 Mack was traded in. The bell was mounted on a custom built stand in October of 1975 and displayed in the department's meeting room and is currently used for ceremonial purposes.

In April of 1975, the department acted to improve the support of our Self Contained Breathing Apparatus. With the use of SCBA at fires and in training increasing rapidly the number of times air bottles need to be filled also increased. It was no longer feasible to have our air bottles filled by air supply equipment of other companies. The department decided to install an air cascade system consisting of three 3500 lb cylinders at a cost of $1,086.80. When full, these large cylinders were capable of filling up to 40 SCBA air bottles. The cascade system was kept filled by Air Unit 328 from the Pikesville Volunteer Fire Company. The system has been upgraded to fill the new 5000 psi air bottles that are now standard for SCBA.

The Glyndon Volunteer Fire Department is continually studying the needs of their community. The department, at that time, was becoming aware of the increasing need for ladder truck service in North West Baltimore County. In 1975, ladder truck service to Glyndon and much of the surrounding area, was provided by the Owings Mills Volunteer Fire Company approximately five miles away.

In July of 1975, President Raymond Warner appointed a committee to investigate the purchase of an aerial ladder truck to add to the department's existing fire suppression units. This committee consisted of Chief James E. Warner, Jr., Cornelius E. Cole, Earl R. Brown, Sr., Richard W. Stem, Jr., Jere Whiteside, James E. Warner, III and President Warner. The committee reported to the department that new ladder trucks cost between $160,000.00 and $225,000.00. These prices exceeded what the department could afford to finance at that time. In addition to purchasing the truck, the department would also have to enlarge the engine room in order to house it.

The committee then began looking for a good, used, piece of equipment with which to start Glyndon's truck company. After investigating many leads for used equipment, and making a number of inspection trips, only to find that the equipment offered did not meet the department's requirements, the committee met with success. In late March of 1976, the committee located a 1960 Peter Pirsch 85 foot ladder truck that was being offered for sale by the Goodwill Volunteer Fire Company of New Castle, Delaware for $30,000.00. On the recommendation of the committee the membership voted to purchase the Goodwill truck. On April 30, 1976, the department placed a deposit of $3,000.00 on Goodwill's truck. The sale was to be completed delivery taken by the department after the delivery of Goodwill's newly ordered aerial.

On October 2, 1976, the balance of $27,000.00 was paid to Goodwill Volunteer Fire Department, and a team consisting of Chief J. Warner, Jr., E. R. Brown, Sr., J. E. Warner, III, J. Whiteside, C. E. Cole and R. Warner, took delivery of the truck, an open cab unit, at Goodwill's quarters and delivered it to the Glyndon station on a very rainy Saturday afternoon. Arriving in Glyndon a little damp, the committee was now faced with the problem of putting a 42' 6" long truck in a 35' firehouse.

The problem was solved temporarily through the generosity of one of our members, Mr. Russell Lessner. When contacted,

Truck 404 1960 Peter Pirsch 85 foot ladder truck, the department's first ladder truck. (GVFD Archives)

Russ generously allowed the truck to be stored in his garage, the old firehouse, on Railroad Avenue for several months while an extension was built to the existing fire station. During this time the truck was readied for service.

As the expansion of the building to house the new truck was being planned, the top of the siren tower was removed using a crane provided by Mr. Bill Pearson, a member of the department. The remainder of the tower was removed as the building expansion progressed. The siren was relocated to the top of the hose tower added to the building as part of the expansion project.

Late in 1976, a committee composed of John A. Warner, Richard W. Stem, Sr., Enoch E. Brown, Sr., E. R. Brown, Sr., Cornelius E. Cole, James E. Warner, Jr., Vernon Gore and President Raymond Warner was appointed to proceed with the Building Expansion Program. On April 5, 1976, the department voted to hire an architect to draft the plans and specifications for the addition to the building. Later that same month, Frank J. Norwicz, Architect, was contracted for the sum of $2,800.00 to provide the drawings and specifications. These architectural drawings were submitted to the company in September of 1976 and bid requests were immediately placed to contractors.

A major requirement placed on the contractors was the ability to begin immediately so space to house the new truck would be available as soon as possible. Work on the truck stored in Russ Lessner's garage was rapidly moving forward and the building expansion needed to be completed so the unit could be placed in service. On September 10, 1976, Jack Mergo Construction Company was contracted to build the first phase of the expansion, an addition that added 8 feet to the front of the apparatus area. Because of zoning problems that needed to be resolved, only this initial phase of the expansion program could be started. The expansion of the front of the building did not add quite enough space to accommodate the full length of the ladder truck. So while the department waited for the zoning approval for the expansion of the rear of the building to be granted one of the windows in the back wall of the engine room was removed and a plywood box built to cover the end of the aerial ladder which protruded several feet beyond the rear wall of the building.

The expansion of the front of the building took place, in part, during the winter. It turned out to be one of the coldest winters in memory. The construction required that the overhead doors in engine room to be removed and replaced by plastic covered 2 x 4 frames. Not only was the engine room very cold that winter but the frames had to be removed from the doors, a two-man job, every time the apparatus responded to an alarm!

On February 18, 1977, with the first phase of the building expansion completed, the new equipment was placed in service as Truck 404 at a total cost of $40,000.00. The first run for Truck 404 was to 415 Valley Meadow Circle on February 21, 1977. On February 18, 1978 Truck 404 ran on a second alarm fire assisting Carroll County fire companies on a building fire at 838 Main Street in Hampstead. The ladder pipe was used for the first time on this fire.

In April of 1977, the Zoning Commission approved the remainder of the expansion project and on September 15, 1977, the O'Meara Construction Company was contracted to complete the expansion project bringing the building to its current form.

The cost of the building expansion project was approximately $125,000.00. The second phase of the new construction consisted of squaring off the rear of building that originally only contained the kitchen. Added to the ground floor, by this addition, were a cloakroom, bar, entryway and two storage rooms. A second story was added above the kitchen that included a new recreation room, workroom, additional apparatus area and a hose tower. The space occupied by the old workroom was used to add 8 feet to the radio room. At the same time, air conditioning was added to the hall at a cost of $8,000.00.

With the building expansion program in 1976-78 and the truck purchase in 1976, the department felt it was not wise to try to purchase a new engine to replace its 20 year old 1959 Mack pumper. Although in good mechanical condition, twenty years of service results in considerable wear on firefighting apparatus. It was becoming increasingly difficult to achieve the required performance standards at the annual pump test.

President Richard Merriken, Sr., in January of 1979, appointed a committee to study the possibility of refurbishing engine 403. This committee was appointed to include Chief Richard W. Stem, Jr., James. E. Warner, Jr., James. E. Warner, III, J. Peter Brach, Jr., Ronnie Merriken, Cleve Armacost and Ted Schultz. The committee was to determine the costs and the feasibility of rebuilding the pump, renovation of the body, replacing the gasoline engine with a diesel engine, and any other updates that might be required to put the equipment in "like new" condition.

In November 1979, after many meetings, the committee decided to solicit bids for refurbishing engine 403. As an alternative, they also looked at a number of used pumpers. None of the used pumpers met the department's requirements and the refurbishing project moved forward.

In August of 1982 Engine 403 developed engine trouble and was removed from service. Reserve Engine 64 was borrowed from the county fire department to temporarily replace engine 403 while repairs were made. The issue of refurbishing the department's 1959 Mack pumper was now, after several years of investigation, brought to a head. A motion was made and carried to re-power engine 403, but not otherwise refurbish it, with a Diesel Engine at a maximum cost of $20,000.

A new refurbishing committee was appointed by President R. Stem, Sr. to include Richard Stem, Jr., Walter Hann, James E. Warner, Jr., Calvin Reter, Gene Cole, Tom Johnson and Richard Stem, Sr.

The committee reviewed the issue of a complete refurbishing of engine 403. They proposed that the department spend an additional $20,000 to complete the refurbishing Engine 403 for a total of $40,000. The proposal was turned over to the Board of Directors for a recommendation. Based on the recommendation of the Board of Directors the department approved an increase in the allocation for re-powering the engine from $20,000 to $22,000 but no funds were approved for the remainder of the refurbishing project.

Engine 403 went to Page-Lambert in McKeesport, PA on October 26, 1982 for re-powering. It was not until December 6, 1982 that the department approved the funds for competing the refurbishing project. Refurbishment was completed on May 27, 1983 at an additional cost of $26,000. The engine, completely refurbished and updated, was put in service on July 9, 1983. Page-Lambert requested, and was granted, permission to take Engine 403 to the Maryland State Firemen's Convention in Ocean City to display their work.

Subsequently, the pump developed problems and was rebuilt to factory specifications completing the long task of refurbishing our venerable 1959 Mack, a task begun in January of 1979 and completed in July of 1983 at a total cost of approximately $51,000.

1979 was a milestone year for the Glyndon Volunteer Fire Department as we celebrated 75 years of community service. President Richard C. Merriken appointed a committee consisting of the following members to plan a gala celebration to commemorate the departments 75th year, President Richard C. Merriken, Sr., James E. Warner, Jr., Mary K. Merriken, Richard Stem, Sr., Richard Cole and C. Leroy Wolfgang.

The celebration was kicked off at our March Annual Awards and Appreciation Banquet with a Multi Media presentation depicting the important events in the department's 75 year history. In September of that year we hosted the annual convention of the Baltimore County Volunteer Firemen's Association Convention.

Historically the Glyndon Volunteer Fire Department has had a policy of incorporating the latest advances in fire fighting technology in our apparatus designs and to upgrade our equipment with the latest proven equipment and appliances. Our initial attack capability was significantly improved by upgrading our 1-1/2" attack lines to 1-3/4" hose that allowed higher water flows without increasing the required pressure. The department also replaced their aging Meushaw hydrant valves with the more efficient Humat hydrant valves at a cost of $1,630. These two changes provided the department with more efficient tools for making the initial attack on interior fires and improved the ability to supply water from the hydrant to the pumper at the fire scene.

On June 23, 1979 a serious fire erupted at Suburban Propane on Old Hanover Road in Woodensburg, Maryland. The fire involved a number of propane tanks on the loading dock and endangered the fleet of propane tank trucks parked nearby as well as a railroad tank car containing a large amount of liquid propane. This is a rural area with no hydrants resulting in multiple alarms being required to establish a water supply for fighting the fire. Mutual aid departments from the surrounding area responded to assist in extinguishing the fire including apparatus from as far away as Baltimore Washington International Airport. The Glyndon Volunteer Fire Department expended almost 1,000 man-hours at the fire.

The addition of ladder truck service by the department in 1977 resulted in a steady increase in our mutual aid responses to neighboring Carroll County. The significant number of mutual aid responses required that the department have the ability to communicate directly with the Carroll County dispatcher and the fire companies operating at fire scenes. To meet this need for improved mutual aid communications the department installed a Carroll County radio in truck 404 in January of 1980.

The Baltimore County Fire Department began a program to provide pagers to each volunteer fire department in the Baltimore County. The pagers responded to the alert tones for each department and allowed the members of the department to be alerted for emergency calls wherever they happened to be. Glyndon received 20 pagers in March of 1980 distributed them to the officers, operators and active members. Over the years the pager program has been expanded to provide each department with pagers for all of its active firefighters.

In July of 1982 Baltimore County began its long awaited Length of Service Awards Program (LOSAP). The Baltimore County Volunteer Firemen's Association, in 1974, proposed the concept of a LOSAP program as an incentive to retain members. The next eight years were spent collecting data and waiting for the county to approve the program and place the required funds in the fire department budget. Members of Baltimore County volunteer fire departments that were over 60 years of age and had been active members of their departments for 25 or more years were eligible to receive $100 per month. The Baltimore County Volunteer Firemen's Association administers

Tower 404 1972 Mack Aerial Scope. (GVFD Photo)

the program for the county through the LOSAP trustees. Richard W. Stem, Sr., a member of the Glyndon Volunteer Fire Department served, as chairman of the LOSAP trustees and currently serves as a member of the board of trustees. Over the years the LOSAP benefit has been increased to the present level of $225 per month. A burial benefit has recently been added to the program.

Three members of the department were certified eligible to receive LOSAP payments in June of 1982. They were Enoch E. Brown, Sr., Richard W. Stem, Sr. and Kenneth F. Mosner. Since that time many members of the department have been certified as eligible for LOSAP and are collecting their benefits. Most are currently active members of the department continuing to serve.

An additional incentive to retain active members was introduced state wide in 1997. The Maryland State Legislature passed a bill providing a state income tax incentive of $3,000 to active members of the state's volunteer fire departments. For Baltimore County departments, the tax incentive program is administered by the LOSAP trustees. The incentive has since been increased to $3500.

The departments venerable metal helmets, the standard of the fire service for many years, went the way of the All Service Gas Mask and Black Cotton Duck Turnout Coats, the victim of improved firefighter safety (they conducted electricity). New, high impact plastic helmets were purchased and the metal helmet passed into history. The change over was completed in February of 1985.

Seeing a need to replace our ladder truck, President Calvin Reter appointed a committee chaired by J. Peter Brach, Jr. with members Ted Schultz, Stephan Hoffnagle, Richard Stem, Sr., Gene Cole, Jim Warner, Jr. and Richard Stem, Jr. to look into the purchase of a newer ladder truck. The committee inspected a number of trucks and finally recommended that the department purchase a 1972 Mack/Baker Tower Ladder (aerialscope) from World Wide Fire Equipment. The unit had seen service with the Fire Department of New York (FDNY) and had been completely refurbished by World Wide Fire Equipment. The department approved the recommendation and on March 17, 1986 moved that the department purchase the truck for $98,800. A $55,000.00 loan was made from the Baltimore County loan fund to put the new truck in service. The Tower Ladder was put in service on July 23, 1986.

Model T Chiefs Car being restored by the department. (GVFD Photo)

The Peter Pirsch Ladder truck was sold to Rock Hall Volunteer Fire Company for $25,000.00 and was delivered on August 2, 1986.

Over the years the department has added equipment to the truck to enhance its ability to perform its mission. The department received a Hurst Tool from a State Grant in November of 1988. Extensive training at the local junkyard (a number of automobiles gave their all to train our crew) was conducted. The addition of this tool to the truck gave the department significantly better capability in auto extrication and rescue. A principal function of the Truck Company is ventilation in support of fire suppression activities. The addition of a new positive pressure ventilation fan to the truck upgraded the department's ability to ventilating smoke filled buildings and to assist in smoke damage prevention as well as supporting firefighting. The fan was placed in service in October of 1990 at a cost of $1,375. A new Honda 6.5 kw unit was purchased in July 1991 for $2,550.00 to replace the second hand generator transferred from the old truck. At the same time the electrical system on the Tower was upgraded to provide fixed floodlights for illumination of emergency scenes.

Some years later the equipment designations were changed to recognize Tower Ladders as being different from straight ladder trucks and in March of 1989 the truck was designated Tower 404.

Hazel and Connie Wolfgang donated a 1924 Model T Fire Chief's Car to the Department in January of 1988. The car had

1989 E-One/Spartan Pumper. (Photo by Joel Woods)

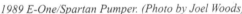

belonged to our deceased member and Past President C. Leroy Wolfgang. He was in the process of restoring the car at the time of his death.

With the truck service successfully upgraded with the purchase of Tower 404 President Calvin Reter appointed a committee consisting of Richard W. Stem, Jr., Richard W. Stem, Sr., James E. Warner, Jr., Edward C. Schultz, Russell Lessner, William Fowble and Chairman, J. Peter Brach, Jr. to purchase a new engine to replace the department's 1959 Mack pumper.

Specifications for a new engine were begun in January of 1988 and were completed and approved by the department in the spring of 1988. The specifications called for a number of advances in apparatus design. A completely enclosed crew cab, air conditioning, and for the first time an automatic transmission was specified. Bids were solicited from the major fire equipment manufacturers and in April of 1989, after a review of the bids, the committee recommended, and department approved the purchase of a 1250 gpm pumper with a 750 gallon water tank from Emergency One of Ocala, Florida to be built on a Spartan chassis for $204,921. Five inch hose and the required special appliances were added to the specifications and purchased separately at a cost of $6,500.

The engine was delivered in November of 1989 and placed in service December 15, 1989. The new Engine 403 was dedicated on May 20, 1990. The 1959 Mack engine was sold to the Pikesville Volunteer Fire Company in April of 1990 for $10,000.

Hollywood came to Glyndon in November of 1988. The department's 1966 Mack pumper was cast in the movie "Her Alibi" starring Tom Sellick. A number of our members became involved in the filming supporting the engine's role. They tell us that Tom was also a supporting actor. Apparently, the scenes featuring our engine were left on the cutting room floor. It would seem that Mr. Sellick did not want any competition from a fire engine.

A major upgrade to the Baltimore County Fire department radio system was completed in November of 1989. The new 800 Mhz communications system vastly improved fire service communications throughout the County.

A Tornado struck the area of Chartley in Reisterstown on Thursday, October 18, 1990. The top floors of several apartment complexes were blown off and numerous homes were damaged in the area of Glyndon Drive, Shirley Manor and Northway Roads. The Tornado seemed to leap to a complex of apartments near Bond Avenue and Glyndon Drive and then to Bond Avenue and the railroad tracks where more homes were damaged extensively. The Glyndon Volunteer

Tornado damage to the Chartley area of Reisterstown. (GVFD Photo)

Fire Department spent 960 man-hours over two days assisting the Reisterstown Volunteer Fire Department in evacuation, lighting and search details. Baltimore County and State Officials arrived quickly to survey the damage. Debris and fallen trees were removed in record time and power was restored to the area by 5:00 PM on Saturday, October 20, 1990.

Public fire safety education, fire prevention, has been a high priority activity of the Glyndon Volunteer Fire Department. The department conducts fire drills at the local schools, conducts fire prevention open houses, and regularly talks to children on the subject of fire safety and prevention. When, in 1992, the Baltimore County Volunteer Firemen's Association and the Baltimore County Fire Department proposed the purchases of a Fire Safety House for use by all of the county fire service organizations the department quickly supported the project and contributed $200 toward its purchase. The house is constructed on a trailer so that it can be easily moved from place to place. The building is designed for use in Fire Prevention for the general public and particularly young people. The department has made good use of the house to bring the message of fire safety and prevention to the community.

The Glyndon Volunteer Fire Department, in March of 1992, began sponsoring Bingo on Thursday nights at the Boring Volunteer Fire Company as a fund raiser to help meet the ever increasing costs of operating the department. The games are conducted by Mason-Dixon Bingo and sponsored by the department. The department had conducted Bingo at the firehouse for many years but the small hall and the requirement to have large prizes made the games unprofitable. Richard Stem, Jr. and his wife Judy were instrumental in establishing the department as a sponsor. The department currently sponsors the games on two nights each week. The steady income from Bingo has made it possible to keep up with the increasing operating expenses and to replace aging apparatus.

The bell from the original firehouse had been loaned to Gill's Church on Walnut Avenue when the current firehouse was constructed. It was returned to the department on June 29, 1990 and put in storage. In September of 1992 the department approved the design and construction of a new sign to be installed in front of firehouse to advertise coming events. The sign was designed to appropriately display the bell from the original firehouse. The bell is an important part of the history of the department and it is now prominently displayed in a place of honor in front of the firehouse. The sign was completed and installed in November of 1992 by Pearson Signs at a cost of $4,168.00.

An Angus Rescue Tool was purchased for $3,995.00 in September of 1992 and mounted on Engine 403. The

The original alarm bell from the old firehouse incorporated in the sign in front of the fire house. (GVFD Photo)

tool is used in rescue operations when the rescue squad or ladder truck is not on the scene.

In June of 1993 the department authorized the purchase of a pickup truck to serve as a Utility Unit. A 1977 Pick-Up Truck was obtained from State surplus property. The vehicle had been used by the Butler Volunteer Fire Company but was no longer needed for their operations. The State surplus property division transferred ownership to the Glyndon Volunteer Fire Department. The pick-up truck was used as a department utility vehicle until 1994 when work began in earnest to build it into a brush unit. The original plan had been to install a skid mount pump and tank to allow the truck to operate as a brush unit during field fire season. The skid mount would be removed at other times to allow use of the truck as a utility vehicle.

This plan was not implemented and when initial work on the unit was completed in June of 1994 it carried only tools and portable tanks for fighting field fires. Medical equipment was added to the vehicle later to support First Responders at medical incidents. The unit was designated as Utility 409. Utility service was formally established by the department in October of 1994 with the receipt of the required approval of the Baltimore County Volunteer Fireman's Association.

Work on Utility 409 continued through 1995 and into 1996 with major work including painting and lettering undertaken by the department. The unit was officially put in service on May 12, 1996.

President Richard W. Stem, Jr. appointed a committee to develop specifications and solicit prices for a new pumper to replace the 1966 Mack (Engine 401). The committee, Chaired by J. Peter Brach, Jr. included Richard W. Stem, Jr., Richard W.

1997 Seagrave 1250 gpm Pumper. (GVFD Photo)

Stem, Sr., Doug Wolfenden, Gene Cole, Kevin Klauza and Paul Wilhelm. Later, James E. Warner, Jr. and Ted Schultz were added to the committee. The committee began work in August of 1994. Preliminary specifications for a new engine were completed in November of 1994 and presented to the department. The original plan was to purchase a tanker/pumper with a 1000 gallon water tank built on a commercial chassis. The estimated cost of the new apparatus was $160,000. Over the next year the committee visited a number departments and inspected apparatus from several manufacturers as plans for the new pumper were developed.

The committee continued working through 1995 fine-tuning plans for the purchase of new apparatus. In March of 1996 Chief Richard W. Stem, Jr. proposed to the committee and President John Amole that the department purchase both a new pumper and a new ladder truck. Tower 404 was aging and maintenance costs were increasing rapidly. The plans then in process for a new pumper would be continued, with specifications for a new ladder truck being developed by the committee. The cost of the pumper was estimated at $200,000 while the ladder truck cost was estimated to be about $400,000. The total cost of the project was estimated to be $600,000 with $400,000 being borrowed from the County apparatus loan fund. A financial analysis by the Treasurer, Richard W. Stem, Sr., supported the project. The Board of Directors approved the project in March of 1996.

The selection of a manufacturer for the ladder truck involved study of the firehouse structure. Door dimensions and floor loading needed to be considered in selecting a design for the ladder truck. The width and height as well as the weight of the apparatus were important criteria in selecting a manufacturer. The Seagrave

1997 Seagrave 100 foot Ladder Truck. (GVFD Photo)

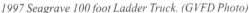

Corporation submitted a proposal fully meeting the apparatus specifications within the dimensional and weight limitations dictated by the firehouse structure.

The apparatus committee reported their selection to the Board of Directors in May of 1996. The Seagave bid included a 100' ladder truck at a cost of $417,000 and a custom pumper with a 1000 gallon water tank, 1250 gpm pump at a cost of $200,000. The board and the department approved the Seagrave bid of $617,000 at a special meeting on June 10, 1996.

The equipment was delivered on October 23, 1997 by a team from the department including John Amole, Paul Wilhelm, Richard Stem, Jr., Richard Stem, Sr., Ted Schultz and James E. Warner, Jr. The equipment was placed in service on February 6, 1998 and formally dedicated on April 25, 1998.

The 1966 Mack, old Engine 401, was sold to the fire department in Theodore, Alabama. Long time member of the department, William Pearson, who now lives in Alabama arranged for the sale. The engine was delivered to Theodore, Alabama by Chief Richard Stem, Jr. and James Warner, Jr. in June of 1996. The apparatus is currently in first line service. (note: as this volume was completed the department learned that the apparatus has been taken out of service)

Tower 404 was placed out of service on November 24, 1997 and offered for sale. The apparatus was sold to the Piney Flats Volunteer Fire Department for $50,000 in August of 1999.

The 1977 pickup truck serving as Utility 409 was worn out! Serious questions were being raised as to its road worthiness and safety. A new utility was an urgent requirement. A committee composed of Chief Richard Stem, Jr., Paul Wilhelm and Assistant Chief Richard Stem, III was charged with the task of developing specifications for a new pickup truck, soliciting prices for vehicles meeting the departments requirements, and making a recommendation to the Board of Directors and the department.

In November of 1999 the committee recommended the purchase of a 2000 Ford F350 4X4 pickup truck with Super Cab and powered by a Diesel engine. The Board approved the purchase and set a cost limit of $35,000 to complete the project. The department approved the Board's recommendation. The new utility, designated Utility 408, was put in service in 2000 and the 1977 pickup was returned to the State. The final cost of the new utility was approximately $45,000.

January 1, 2000 brought the last year of the 20th Century. There was great concern that the year transition from 1999 to 2000 would result in wide spread failure of computer systems resulting in serious disruption of essential services including emergency services. The Glyndon Volunteer Fire

Utility 408, 2000 Ford F350 4x4 Pick-up Truck. (GVFD Photo)

Department manned the station in the event of a failure of the dispatching system. Nothing happened... The New Year was rung in with elaborate celebrations around the world... with out incident. To everyone's relief Y2K never happened!

The country was not so lucky in 2001, the first year of the new millennium. On September 11, 2001 terrorists attacked the United States of America causing a large loss of life. Two commercial airliners were flown into the twin towers of the World Trade Center in New York City. In addition to a large number of civilian deaths 343 members of the Fire Department of New York (FDNY) gave their lives when the Towers collapsed. A third airliner was flown into the Pentagon while a forth crashed in Pennsylvania as a result of the action of the passengers preventing an attack on another building probably in Washington D.C.

September 11, 2001 was a beautiful, sunny, late summer day. Americans went about their daily routines with the sense of security and safety they were accustomed to and took for granted. At approximately 8:45 AM that day, every thing changed. American Airlines Flight 11 from Boston to Los Angeles was flown into the North Tower of New York City's World Trade Center with 92 passengers and crew members on board. Although we did not know it at the time we were under attack. The North Tower burst into flames. Firefighters and emergency workers rushed to the tower to save as many as possible from the burning upper floors of the building. The day of horror was just beginning.

At approximately 9:10 AM United Airlines Flight 175 was flown into the South Tower of the World Trade Center with 56 passengers and 9 crew members aboard. It was apparent that this was not an accident but a terrorist attack. Mayor Rudolf Giuliani took immediate action. All transportation into the city of New York was shut down, as well as, all bridges and tunnels between New York and New Jersey.

The South Tower of the World Trade Center, the second of the two towers to be attacked, collapsed at 10:05 AM. Clouds of dust and debris came crashing to the ground. The rescuers, firefighters and police, who had been working to save as many of the building's occupants as possible were trapped with many of the people they were trying to save. The North Tower of the World Trade Center collapsed at 10:28 AM less than half an hour after the South Tower again trapping rescuers and victims. The city of New York was enveloped in a cloud of dust that could be seen for miles. The official death toll for the World Trade Center attack has been set at 2,749 souls. FDNY lost 343 brothers, 75 law enforcement officers were killed that day.

The city of New York was not the only target of the terrorists. At approximately 9:43 AM, American Airlines Flight 77 from Washington to Los Angeles crashed into the Pentagon with 58 passengers and six crew members on board. On the ground, 124 men and women were killed. The Pentagon was evacuated immediately. The State and Justice departments were shut down and all federal office buildings in Washington were evacuated.

United Airlines Flight 93 departing from Newark, NJ to San Francisco was in flight when the passengers learned about the attacks on New York City. Passengers were able to divert the Boeing 757 from its intended target saving many lives while sacrificing their own. This flight crashed in a field in Shanksville PA at approximately 10:13 AM killing all 40 passengers and crewmembers on board.

Emergency workers responded in large numbers to the attack sites to assist in any way they could. Rescue workers searched for survivors with all the resources at their disposal in hope that survivors would be found. As night fell, the fires at the World Trade Center still burned and continued to burn for 99 days. Few survivors were found.

On September 13, 2001 the President held a press conference and vowed that the United States would hunt down those responsible the terrorist acts of September 11, 2001. The war on terrorism had begun and the fire service would, as they had in the past, rise to meet the challenges this war would bring. New and unfamiliar threats were addressed. Weapons of Mass Destruction, Bio-terrorism, and mass casualty incidents joined more conventional fire and rescue topics at department training drills. The Glyndon Volunteer Fire Department is meeting the challenge of protecting the community from these new threats as it did from those of conventional warfare in 1918, 1941 and through the years of the cold war.

The department had been evaluating its emergency responses for a number of years to determine its future apparatus requirements. The number of calls that did not require the response of an engine or truck such as medical boxes, lockout details and first responder calls to assist the medical units were increasing significantly. Most of these calls could be handled by two firefighters responding with an appropriately equipped piece of apparatus and did not, in most cases, require an engine or truck response.

In February of 2002 the department approved the addition of a Special Unit equipped to handle the growing number of non-fire related calls. The unit would operate with a crew of two and would be equipped to handle many different types of emergencies. The cost of the Special Unit would be covered by the sale of one of the department's pumpers.

President Ted Schultz appointed a committee consisting of Chief Scott Warner, Jim Warner, Jr. and the President to investigate the purchase of a Special Unit. The committee inspected units at the Pikesville Volunteer Fire Company and the Owings Mills Volunteer Fire Company. The Pikesville equipment needed considerable renovation to meet the requirements established by the committee. The Owings Mills unit, a 1994 Ford F450 4x4 Special Unit, met the department's requirements and was initially offered at a price of $85,000.

In August of 2002 the department approved the sale of the Spartan/E-One engine (E-403) to the Blue Ridge Mountain Volunteer Fire Company No. 5, Harpers Ferry, West Virginia for $76,840. The proceeds from the sale were used to purchase the Owing Mills Volunteer Fire Company Special Unit for $50,000 in September 2002. The equipment was delivered on January 29, 2003.

The unit, as delivered was painted in the Owings Mills bright Yellow color scheme. Painting was an immediate requirement. A number of bids were solicited for the paint job. Delmarva Fire Equipment was the winning bidder and the unit was sent to their shop on March 2, 2003. The Special Unit, now designated SU 407, was delivered to the Glyndon station on April 2, 2003 painted red, as fire equipment should be. The next two months were spent mounting equipment and training personnel. Chief Warner placed the Special Unit in service on June 2, 2003. The total cost of the unit including $11,500 for painting, and $4,221 for equipment was $65,721 well below the budget of $70,000.

The firehouse, which for many years, had served the department's needs well, requiring only occasional maintenance, was in need of renovation. In 1976/1977 the engine room was expanded to accommodate the ladder truck. A recreation room and additions to the hall were built as well. A new workroom was added and the watch room enlarged as part of this project.

By 1993 the management demands on the suppression and administrative officers of the department had increased considerably. The need for office space for the officers was critical. In August of 1993, the department approved the first of a number of renovations to the firehouse that would take place over the years. A bunkroom, workroom and a shared office for the suppression and administrative officers were added to the building.

In May of 2001 additional changes to the building were made to provide separate offices for the administrative and suppression officers. Again, the changes were accomplished by changing the interior arrangement of the building. The second floor of the building received much needed air conditioning for the offices, watch room, bunkroom and recreation room as part of this project.

For ten years the department used a band-aid approach to meeting its space needs. Fire apparatus has become larger in this time and the engine room last renovated in 1976/1977 is barely adequate for housing our present apparatus.

In 2003 President Ted Schultz appointed a committee with the following members: Ted Schultz, Chairman; James E. Warner, Jr., Chief Scott Warner, Rick Cole, Casey Caples and Scott Rudow to develop plans for a major improvement and expansion of the building. The committee focused on a number of concerns including additional space for apparatus, a larger social hall, improved office space, crew sleeping quarters, and general updating of the building infrastructure.

An Architect was hired and preliminary plans were developed and presented to the department. The plans included additional apparatus bays with

Special Unit 407, 1994 Ford F450 4x4 Special Unit. (GVFD Photo)

higher and wider doors to accommodate larger apparatus. A larger hall was included in the plan along with improvements to the office space, bunkroom and storage. The exterior appearance of the building was also changed to make it more attractive to the community.

The initial plans for expanding the firehouse would have required the department's rental property to be razed. This resulted in some controversy with the community. The property is in need of substantial costly repair and renovation and the building expansion committee felt the most cost effective use of the property was to raze the building and expand the firehouse in its place. The department is working closely with the community to arrive at a plan that will allow the building to meet the future needs of the department and present the community with an attractive structure. The committee is currently searching for viable means to save the house and possibly integrate it into the planned expansion. A number of options are being considered to allow the department to achieve its space requirements while retaining the rental property structure. The work of this committee is ongoing and at present has not developed a definitive plan for meeting the objectives that will take the department into its second century of service to the Glyndon community.

In the late 1980s computer technology was introduced to the department when the Ladies Auxiliary purchased a computer for the department. The department utilized the new technology to maintain many of the department's records. As computer technology advanced the first computer committee chairman, Marty Listwan, kept the department up to date by arranging to upgrade our computer equipment when needed.

The Baltimore County Volunteer Firemen's Association initiated a program to supply computer equipment and a high-speed connection to the Internet to each volunteer fire department in

Architect's concept drawing of one option for expansion of the firehouse.

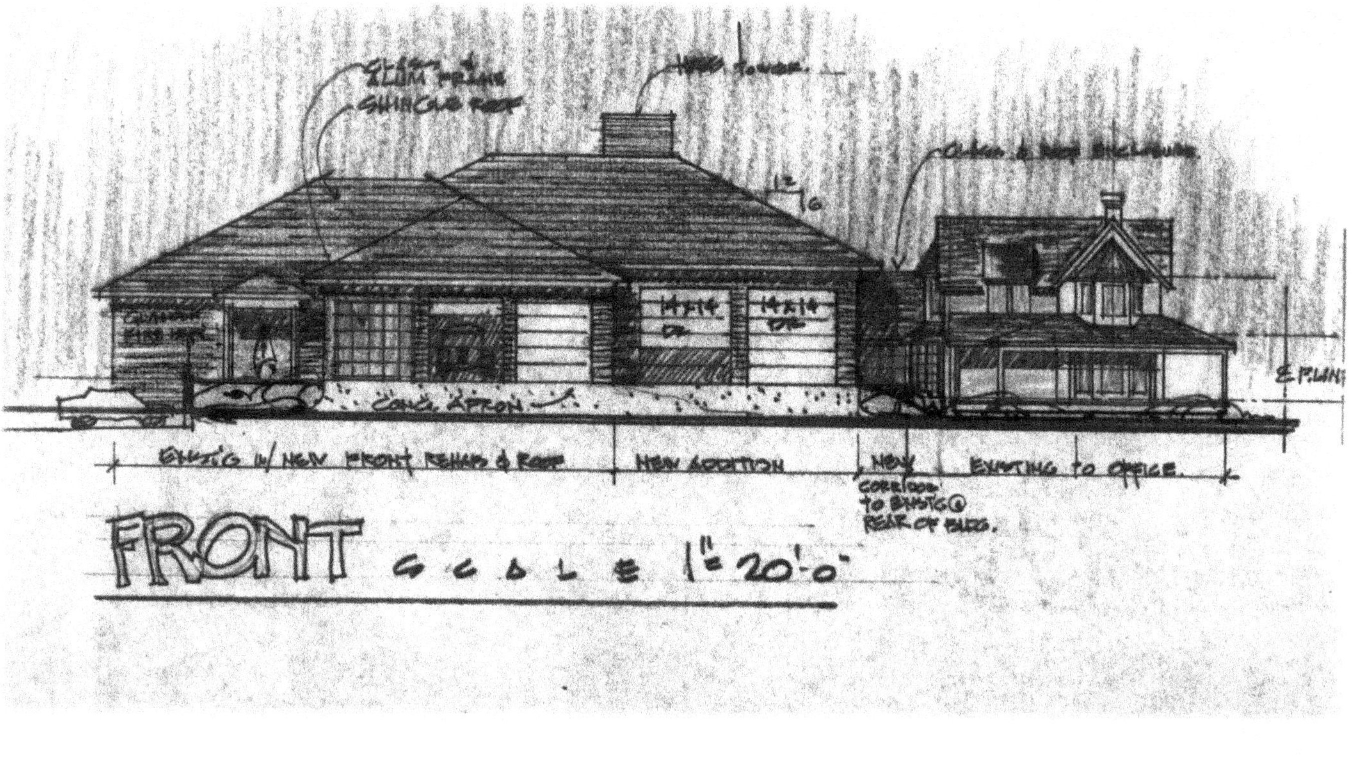

the county. Although The Glyndon Volunteer Fire Department had been using computers for their day-to-day management for some time they did not have access to the Internet. In May of 2000 the county computer was installed at the firehouse and access to the computer and the Internet was provided to all of our members.

With the value of computers to the department's operation solidly established the department approved the purchase of a new Gateway computer for the administration. A new Dell computer was purchased for the suppression a short time later. With the help of Marty Listwan and the department's computer coordinator J. Peter Brach, Jr. a Local Area Network (LAN) was established at the firehouse connecting the department's three computers to the high speed Internet connection.

The value of the Internet to the department as a tool for training and research, and as a vehicle to promote the department had been established. Glyndon joined many of the departments in Baltimore County and nation wide in developing a web site. Marty Listwan was appointed Web Master and developed a spectacular website which may be viewed and enjoyed by everyone at **www.gvfd40.org.** The site contains information about the department as well as contact information and photographs of the department's apparatus, activities and emergency responses. The site also serves the members by providing notices of meetings, training schedules, membership information and individual E-Mail accounts for members who wish them. Interest in the site has been high with the number of visitors steadily increasing.

The Franklin Station (Station 56) of the Baltimore County Fire Department began operations on November 7, 2003 bring-

Franklin Station 56 Baltimore County Fire Department. (GVFD Photo)

ing career emergency services to the Reisterstown/Glyndon area. The new station houses Engine 56 and Medic 56 and provides much needed full time assistance to the Volunteer Fire Departments in North West Baltimore County. Extensive growth in the area was beginning to tax the ability of the fully volunteer fire and rescue departments that have been serving the communities of North West Baltimore County for over 100 years to provide high quality service particularly during weekday working hours.

Throughout its 100 years of community service, the members of the Glyndon Volunteer Fire Department have striven to provide the most modern and effective fire protection possible to the residents of the Glyndon Community. This chronicle details the growth of this department from one horse drawn rig housed in a borrowed building, pulled by livery horses, to a modern fire fighting force with four pieces of apparatus carefully chosen to meet the special needs of the people it serves. This remarkable growth has only been possible through the self-sacrifice of all of the members, past and present, and through the constant and generous support of the residents of Glyndon.

Special recognition must go to the generous contributions of the Ladies Auxiliary to the Glyndon Volunteer Fire Department. Without their support the department would never have been able to provide the community with the fire suppression services that are now available.

It is the intent of the Glyndon Volunteer Fire Department, with the continued support of the Glyndon community, to provide the best possible fire protection and community service possible, and to continue its policy of the last 100 years of always looking to the future needs of the community it serves.

Engine 56 Baltimore County Fire Department. (GVFD Photo)

The Apparatus

GLYNDON Volunteers
LADDER 404
GLYNDON
GLYNDON VOLUNTEER FIRE DEPT

Apparatus Notebook

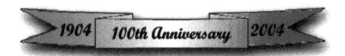

1904 100th Anniversary 2004

In its 100 year history the Glyndon Volunteer Fire Department has owned 15 pieces of major fire apparatus, one hand drawn chemical engine, four brush/utility units and one Special Unit. With the exception of the 1913 White Maxwell engine for which a photograph was not available and Utility 409, which is pictured here, each of these pieces of apparatus has been described and a photograph provided in "Answering the Call." Here we will attempt to show how some of our modern apparatus evolved and changed to meet the needs of the community and what happened to it when we replaced it with updated or new equipment. Where we were able, we contacted the new owners of the equipment and asked them to send us photographs showing how it looks today. As you will see one piece of our apparatus had an interesting and varied career after it left Glyndon. Our purpose here is to provide interesting vignettes of our apparatus as it evolved to meet the needs of the Glyndon community and how they went on to serve other communities.

1937 Ford Engine

The 1937 Ford was purchased from Beall Motors for $588.00 and remained in service until 1961 when it was replaced by a 1951 Dodge Power Wagon and sold to F. L Anderson Co. for $500.00.

The 1937 Ford was quickly equipped to serve as a ladder truck with the addition of a longer extension ladder and fittings that allowed it to be raised from the rear step.

The ladder arrangement did not work as well as hoped and was subsequently removed. The engine was later equipped with a portable pump and field fire fighting equipment and served as a field and brush fire unit until replaced in 1961.

1937 Ford with ladder mounted to rear step and extended in the operating position. Firefighter on ladder is unidentified. (GVFD Archives)

1937 Ford with extension ladder mounted a rack over the body. (GVFD Archives)

Close-up of the 1937 Ford with ladder rack removed. Note Indian Tanks on running board for fighting field and brush fires. (GVFD Archives)

The Macks

Beginning in 1947, the department began a long association with Mack Fire Apparatus, which resulted in the purchase of three engines. The first, the 1947 Mack was purchased to replace the 1928 American La France and remained in service until 1966.

In1959 a new Mack engine, designated Engine 403, was purchased at a cost of $26,800 giving the department two first line pumpers. This piece of equipment represented the state-of-the-art in modern fire equipment. It was the first of its design in Baltimore County. Equipped with an 800-gallon water tank and 750 gallon-per-minute (gpm) Hale pump, it was designed to serve the needs of the mostly rural Glyndon community. The "cab forward" design was acquired from the Ahrens Fox Fire Apparatus Company by the Mack Truck Company and was to become a "classic" in fire apparatus design. As our photo history will show this piece of equipment "got around."

Close-up of the 1937 Ford showing ladder rack mounted over the hose body and cab. Note boot racks on the side of the apparatus. (GVFD Archives)

The engine was completely refurbished in 1982. As part of this project the two booster reels were reduced to one and relocated to provide space for the cross-lay attack lines. The number of suction sleeves was reduced to two. The unit was re-powered with a diesel engine and the pump was later rebuilt providing several years of additional service to the department.

Engine 403 was replaced in 1989 with an Emergency-one/Spartan engine. The 1959 Mack was sold to the Pikesville Volunteer Fire Company. The Pikesville Company converted it for service as a rescue unit while they awaited delivery of a new Squad.

The story does not end here. The Pikesville Volunteer Fire Company sold the unit to the Baltimore County Fire Department. The BCFD converted the engine for use as a Fire Safety Education unit. The BCFD later consigned the piece to an auction company for sale. The Glyndon Volunteer Fire Department re-purchased the engine for $4000 with the thought of restoring it for use at parades.

The department was unable to find a place to store the engine while restoration work was being done so it was decided that the best course of action was to sell the piece rather than let the weather take its toll. The engine was sold to George Cowman for $5000. The engine has been

1947 Mack engine in front of engine house. (GVFD Archives)

completely restored as a memorial to 9/11 and is frequently seen in local parades.

In 1966 the department replaced the aging 1947 Mack with the twin of the 1959 engine at a cost of $30,368 continuing the "Mack lineage." The apparatus was diesel powered with a 750 gpm Waterous pump and a 750 gallon water tank and was designated as Engine 401. The engine remained in service until replaced in 1997 with a Seagrave pumper.

Major modifications were made to Engine 401 to improve firefighting efficiency. The booster reels were completely removed and cross-lay attack lines added. The number of suction sleeves was reduced to two.

The engine was sold to the St. Elmo – Irvington Volunteer Fire Department of Theodore, Alabama. William Pearson, GVFD life member and current member of the St. Elmo – Irvington Volunteer Fire Department was instrumental in arranging the sale. Chief Richard Stem, Jr. and past Chief James E. Warner, Jr. delivered the piece to the St Elmo – Irvington VFD and trained the department's members in its operation.

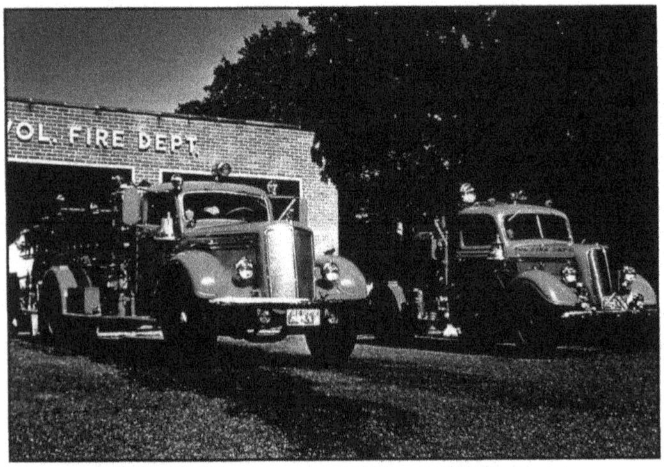

1947 Mack engine with 1937 Ford. (GVFD Photo)

1959 Mack, Engine 403, as delivered to the department. (Photo by Joel Woods)

1959 Mack after refurbishing. Note revised engine compartment, reduced number of suction sleeves, single booster reel and cross-lay attack lines. (Photo by Joel Woods)

The 1959 Mack as a rescue unit in service at the Pikesville Volunteer Fire Company. (Photo Courtesy PVFC)

The 1959 Mack as the BCFD Fire Education Unit. (GVFD Photo)

The 1959 Mack, restored by George Cowman. Note the chrome wheels and superb paint job. (GVFD Photo)

1966 Mack, Engine 401 as delivered to the department. (Photo by Joel Woods)

Engine 401 showing minor changes to the equipment lay out. Note relocated fire extinguisher. Fittings over pump panel were moved to compartment. (Photo by Joel Woods)

Engine 401 after major modifications to remove the booster reels and add cross-lay attack lines. (GVFD Photo)

The 1966 Mack in service at the St. Elmo – Irvington Volunteer Fire Department. Standing in front of the engine are William Pearson (L) and another member of the St. Elmo Fire Department. (GVFD Photo)

E-One/Spartan committee (L to R) Ted Schultz, Chairman J. Peter Brach, Jr., James E. Warner, Jr., Bill Fowble, Richard W. Stem, Jr., Richard W. Stem, Sr., not in photograph Russell Lessner. (GVFD Photo)

The End of an Era

An Emergency-One engine on a Spartan chassis was purchase in 1989 at a cost of $204,921 as a replacement for the 1959 Mack. And thus ended the reign of the "Macks" at the Glyndon Volunteer Fire Department as first line engines. The E-One again represented the state-of-the-art in fire apparatus. It sported a ten man cab allowing all of the firefighters to ride inside, a major improvement in safety. The hose bed was designed to accept 5 inch Large Diameter Hose. A 1250 gpm pump and 750 gallon water tank recognized the changing character of the area served by the department. Several shopping Malls and an increase in the number of apartment required the increase in pump capacity and the move to LDH, while the area without municipal water still required large water tanks. The engine was placed in service in December of 1989.

In August of 2002 Engine 403 was sold to the Blue Ridge Mountain Volunteer Fire Company No. 5 of Harpers Ferry, West Virginia for $74,840. For the first time in 55 years the Glyndon Volunteer Fire Department was operating as a single engine department. The proceeds from the sale of Engine 403 were used to purchase a special unit. These changes reflected changes in fire protection needs and manpower availability.

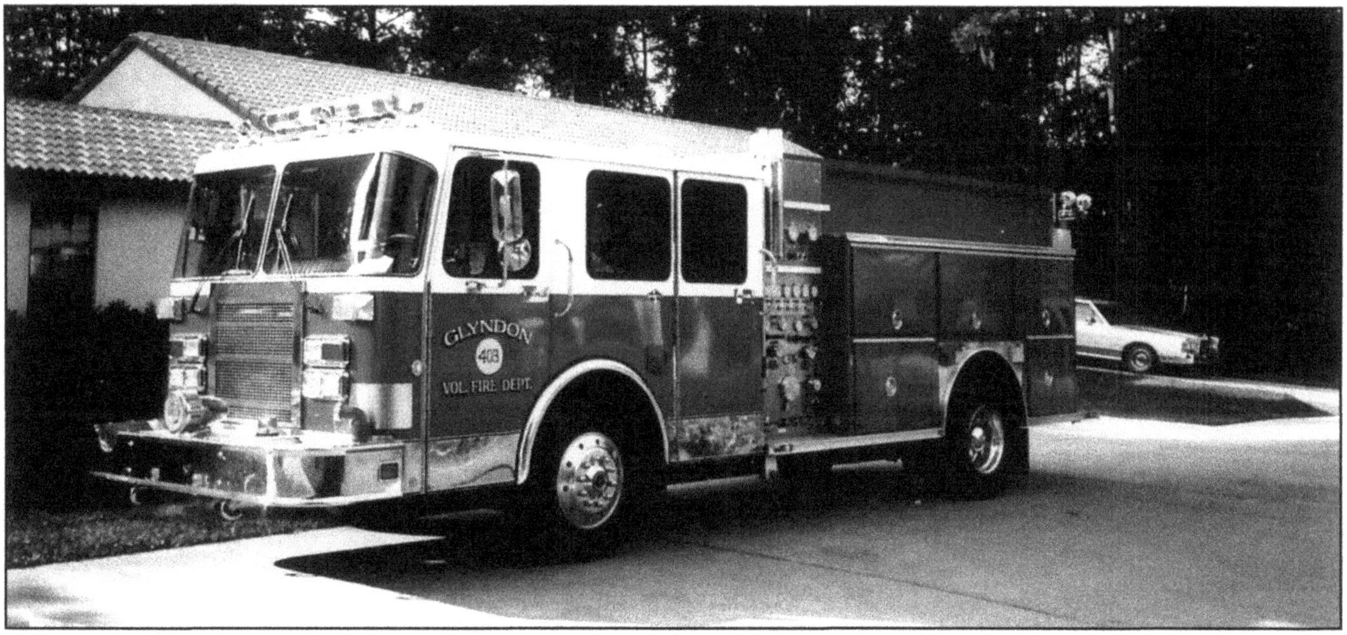

1989 E-One/Spartan at Emergency-One, Ocala, Florida. (GVFD Photo)

Committee Chairman J. Peter Brach, Jr. places new Engine 403 in service at dedication ceremonies. (GVFD Photo)

New Engine 403 in service. Note lettering and department patch added after delivery. (Photo by Joel Woods)

E-One/Spartan in service at the Blue Ridge Mountain Volunteer Fire Company No.5, Harpers Ferry, West Virginia. (GVFD Photo)

THE TRUCKS

The first of the modern Ladder Trucks was a 1960 Peter Pirsch 85 foot Ladder purchased in 1977 from the Goodwill Volunteer Fire Company of New Castle Delaware at a cost of $30,000. The Truck was replaced with a Mack/Baker Aerial Scope in 1986 and sold to the Rock Hall Volunteer Fire Department for $25,000. A member of the Rock Hall department, with the intent of restoring the piece, subsequently purchased the Truck. Finding that restoration was more costly than originally thought the truck was sold to Paul Jones of Clayton, Delaware in whose field it is currently parked.

Ladder Truck service at the Glyndon Volunteer Fire Department underwent a major upgrade with the purchase, in 1986, of a 1972 Mack/Baker 75 foot Aerial Scope from World Wide Fire Equipment. World Wide Fire Equipment refurbished the Truck, which was originally in service with the Fire Department of New York City (FDNY).

1960 Peter Pirsch Ladder Truck. (Photo by Joel Woods)

Tower 404 Committee. (L to R) Richard W. Stem, Jr., James E. Warner, Jr., Chairman J. Peter Brach, Jr., Richard W. Stem, Sr., C. E. "Gene" Cole, Ted Schultz, not in photograph Stephen Hoffnagle. (GVFD Photo)

The Tower was replaced in 1997 with a 100-foot Seagrave Ladder Truck. The Tower was subsequently sold, in 1999, to the Piney Flats Volunteer Fire Department (Tennessee) for $50,000. While the Tower was being demonstrated to the representatives of the Piney Flats department a hydraulics failure occurred and the Tower toppled on to its side. There were no injuries and the damage, which was not serious, was quickly repaired and the sale completed.

1960 Peter Pirsch Ladder Truck rusting away in current owners field. An ignominious end for a proud piece of fire apparatus. (GVFD Photo)

Tower 404 with bucket fully extended. (GVFD Photo)

1972 Mack/Baker Aerial Scope designated Tower 404. (GVFD Photo)

Tower 404 on its side after hydraulics failure occurred. (GVFD Photo)

Tower in service at the Piney Flats Volunteer Fire Department. (Photo Courtesy Piney Flats VFD)

John Amole (L) with Chief Richard W. Stem, Jr. places Engine 401 in service at dedication ceremonies. (GVFD Photo)

Two at Once

In 1996 the department approved the purchase of two major pieces of apparatus from the Seagrave Corporation. A contract was signed for a 100-foot Ladder Truck at a cost of $417,000 to replace Tower 404. A new engine with a 1250 gpm pump and a 1000-gallon water tank, to replace Engine 401, and costing $200,000, was ordered at the same time. This single purchase replaced a 30-year-old Engine and a 24-year-old Truck bringing all of the department's apparatus the latest standards.

Calvin Reter (L) and James E. Warner, Jr. place Truck 404 in service at dedication ceremonies. (GVFD Photo)

1997 Seagrave Truck 404 and Engine 401 in front of the station. (GVFD Photo)

Engine/Truck committee. (L to R) Ted Schultz, Richard W. Stem, Jr., James E. Warner, Jr., Paul Wilhelm, John Flannery, Richard W. Stem, Sr. John Amole, Chairman J. Peter Brach, Jr. Not in photograph Kevin Klausa. (GVFD Photo)

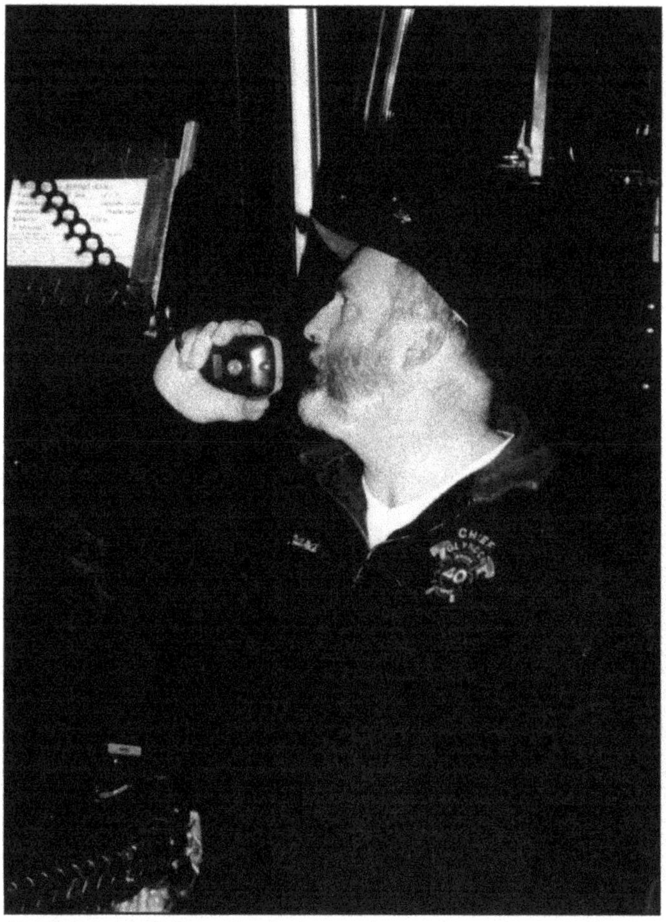

Chief Richard W. Stem, Jr. placing equipment in service at dedication ceremonies. (GVFD Photo)

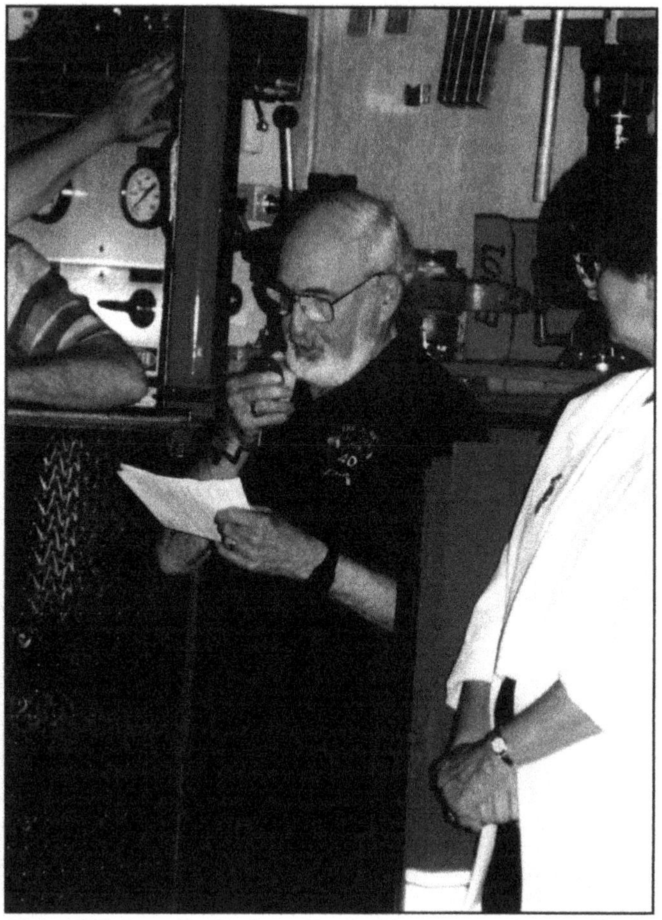

Richard W. Stem, Sr. (L) places Truck 404 in service. Joan Wolfenden looks on. (GVFD Photo)

Chief Scott Warner places SU 407 in service at dedication ceremonies. (GVFD Photo)

Special and Utility Vehicles

The introduction of Special Unit 407 reflected changes that have occurred in the role the fire department plays in servicing the community. Over the last few years the number of medical assistance calls the department responds to has increased substantially as has the number of utility calls such as carbon monoxide detector alarms and smoke detector alarms with no fire. The Special unit is also equipped for light rescue work.

Special Unit 407 began life with the nearby Owings Mills Volunteer Fire Company. Painted yellow and still bearing the Owings Mills markings of its previous owner it was delivered to the Glyndon Volunteer Fire Department in January of 2003. The price was $50,000. Newly painted and equipped to meet GVFD requirements SU 407 was placed in service in June of 2003. The total cost: $65,721.

Last but not by any means least, are the Utility vehicles. The first was a 1977 pick up truck obtained through the State Surplus Property Division. The unit had been in service at the Butler Volunteer Fire Department and was transferred to Glyndon in1993. Utility 408, a 1999 Ford 350 4x4 pickup truck, replaced it. The new Utility unit is an important vehicle carrying members to meetings and training classes as well as responding to medical assistance and utility calls.

SU 407, looking like large canary, is delivered by the Owings Mills Volunteer Fire Company. (GVFD Photo)

SU 407 repainted and in service for the Glyndon Volunteer Fire Department. (GVFD Photo)

Special Unit committee at dedication. (L to R) Chief Scott Warner, BCFD Chief John Hohman, James E. Warner, Jr. and Ted Schultz. (GVFD Photo)

Utility 408, 1999 Ford 350 4x4 pick up truck. (GVFD Photo)

Utility 409, 1977 Dodge Pick up truck. (GVFD Photo)

Looking Back

Five photographs show the continuing effort of the Glyndon Volunteer Fire Department to protect the Glyndon community with the most modern and efficient fire equipment available. These photographs show the mix of equipment operated by the Glyndon Volunteer Fire Department over the years and the department's dedication to meeting the needs of the community with the best apparatus available.

(L to R) 1951 Dodge Power Wagon Brush unit, 1947 Mack engine, 1959 Mack engine. The station shown in this photo is as it was originally constructed. (GVFD Archives)

(From Bottom of Photo) International Scout, 1966 Mack engine, 1989 E-one engine, Tower 404. (GVFD Photo)

(L to R) 1989 E-one engine, 1972 Mack/Baker Aerial Scope, 1966 Mack engine. (GVFD Photo)

(From the bottom of photo) 1972 International Scout Brush unit, 1959 Mack engine, 1966 Mack engine, 1960 Peter Pirsch Ladder Truck. (GVFD Archives)

(L to R) 1997 Seagrave engine, 1989 E-One engine, 1997 Seagave Ladder Truck. (GVFD Photo)

The Members and Officers

The Members and Officers of The Glyndon Volunteer Fire Department

1904 100th Anniversary 2004

100 Years of Leadership and Service

1904

The founding officers of the Department, selected at the first official meeting of the fledgling fire company, on March 25, 1904 were:

President:	J. Smith Orrick
Chief Foreman:	Geo. H. Taylor
1st Vice President:	Chas. R. McNeal
1st Ass't Foreman:	Chas. B. Kelly
2nd Vice President:	J. J. Dyer
2nd Ass't Foreman:	Chas. E. Sentz
Secretary:	W. T. Stringer
Marshal:	Wm. Chineworth
Treasurer:	T. Reese Arnold
Ass't Marshal:	Geo. A. Schull
Ass't Secretary:	C. C. Billmyer
Librarian:	C. H. Whittle
Janitor:	Grover C. Danner

Twenty-three men from the Glyndon community attended that historic meeting and volunteered to help protect their town. The records show these dedicated men to be:

J. Smith Orrick	C. C. Billmyer
Chas. R. McNeal	Chas. B. Kelly
J. J. Dyer	Geo. E. Smith
T. Reese Arnold	J. H. Lohr
Geo. H. Taylor	Chas. Switzer
Chas. E. Sentz	A. M. Ruby
Wm. Chineworth	D. Danner
Geo. A. Schull	Henry Baublitz
C. H. Whittle	Ernest Benson
G. G. Dausser	Albert Henry
A. A. Rich	T. Whittle
W. T. Stringer	

We know almost nothing about most of these men. They came from all walks of life and included a judge, J. Smith Orrick; a teacher and Civil Servant, T. Reese Arnold; and a number of local businessmen including Chas. B. Kelly who operated the local blacksmith shop. They had a common bond; regardless of their place in the community, they were dedicated to serving it.

Three of the first officers of the newly formed fire company left us an invaluable legacy, their photographs and for two of the departments first officers mini biographies.

Judge J. Smith Orrick was the first president of the Fire Company. In addition to his likeness the back of his photograph tells us the following:

> "Judge J. Smith Orrick. First President of the Glyndon Vol. Fire Co. Long resident of Glyndon...many years as Justice of the Peace. First President of the Glyndon Permanent Building Association. Vestryman of All Saints Episcopal Church."

Mr. W. Taylor Stringer was the first Secretary of the Fire Company. Unfortunately we were given no biographical information with his photograph. However the minutes of the first years of the Companies existence are recorded in his beautiful Victorian scrip with many marginal notes in classic Gregg shorthand.

Mr. Thomas Reese Arnold was the first Treasurer of the Fire Company an office he held until his death in 1914. Mr. Arnold was born in Staunton, Virginia in 1850 and moved to Glyndon about 1870. He was a schoolteacher for a number of years before working for the Federal Government under Civil Service. At the time of his death, he was Chief Clerk to the Appraiser of the Port of Baltimore. The high regard in which Mr. Arnold was held by the Fire Company is expressed in just a few lines from a tribute written on the occasion of his death by Mr. J. Henry Albrecht, a member of the Fire Company.

"We firemen will miss him, whose laugh we all knew
May his soul rest in peace at God's will,
We mourn his great loss, and his family console
There's no one that place can fill."

Judge J. Smith Orrick
First President, Glyndon Volunteer Fire Company
(GVFD Archives)

W. Taylor Stringer
First Secretary of the Glyndon Volunteer Fire Company
(GVFD Archives)

Thomas Reese Arnold
First Treasurer of the Glyndon Volunteer Fire Company
GVFD Archives

2004

One hundred years later another group of dedicated men, and this time women, assumed the leadership of the Glyndon Volunteer Fire Department. The officers for the centennial year are:

Administrative Officers

President:	Edward "Ted" Schultz
1st Vice President:	Scott Rudow
2nd Vice President:	Kathy Wolfenden
Recording Secretary:	Dorothy Schultz
Corresponding Secretary:	Kathy Reitz
Treasurer:	Richard W. Stem, Sr.
Assistant Treasurer:	Frank Renard
Chaplain:	Norman Obenshain
Assistant Chaplain:	Joan Wolfenden

Suppression Officers

Chief:	Scott Warner
Assistant Chief:	Doug Wolfenden
Captain:	Randy Brown
Lieutenant:	Justin McCracken
Lieutenant:	Ronnie Mintz
Lieutenant:	John Rice
Lieutenant:	Charles Webster

Board of Directors

Chairman:	James E. Warner, Jr.
President:	Edward "Ted" Schultz
Chief:	Scott Warner
	Justin McCracken
	Scott Rudow
	Richard W. Stem, Sr.
	Doug Wolfenden

Installation of Officers

The administrative and suppression officers for the year 2004 were installed at ceremonies held on January 12, 2004. The community was invited to attend the ceremonies and share this historic event with the members of the Glyndon Volunteer Fire Department.

(Left) Joel McCrea, President of the Baltimore County Volunteer Firemen's Association, installs the administrative officers for the year 2004. (Photo by Bernard J. Roche)

(Right) Administrative officers for the year 2004. Seated (L to R) Joan Wolfenden, Assistant Chaplain; Kathy Reitz, Corresponding Secretary; Kathy Wolfenden, 2nd Vice President; Dorothy Schultz, Recording Secretary. Standing (L to R) Richard W. Stem, Sr. Treasurer; Frank Renard, Assistant Treasurer; Pastor Norman Obenshain, Chaplain; Scott Rudow, 1st Vice President; Edward "Ted" Schultz, President. (Photo by Bernard J. Roche)

Board of Directors for the year 2004. (L to R) Richard W. Stem, Sr., Scott Rudow, Chief Scott Warner, Assistant Chief Doug Wolfenden, President Edward "Ted" Schultz, James E. Warner, Jr., Chairman. (Photo by Bernard J. Roche)

John Hohman, Chief of the Baltimore County Fire Department, installs the suppression officers for the year 2004. (Photo by Bernard J. Roche)

Suppression officers for the year 2004. (L-R) Lieut. John Rice, Lieut. Ronnie Mintz, Lieut. Charles Webster. Captain Randy Brown, Assistant Chief Doug Wolfenden and Chief Scott Warner. Not in photo: Lieut. Justin McCracken. (Photo by Bernard J. Roche)

100 Years of Leadership of
The Glyndon Volunteer Fire Department
1904 – 2004

Senior Officers 1904 – 2004

The Glyndon Volunteer Fire Department proudly recognizes the members who have served with distinction as its leaders for the past 100 years. These men have lead the department from its earliest days guiding it on a path of steady growth to the modern, efficient department that protects the town of Glyndon today.

	President	Chief Foreman
1904	J. Smith Orrick	George Taylor
1905	J. Smith Orrick	George Taylor
1906	J. Smith Orrick	Charles B. Kelly
1907	J. Smith Orrick	Charles B. Kelly
1908	C. R. McNeal	Charles Sentz
1909	C. R. McNeal	Charles Sentz
1910	C. R. McNeal	No Record
1911	No Record	No Record
1912	C. H. Whittle	No Record
1913	C. H. Whittle	Lester Wheeler
1914	C. H. Whittle	A. W. Fuss
1915	C. H. Whittle	William Royston
1916	C. H. Whittle	G. E. Penn
1917	C. H. Whittle	Walter Snyder
1918	C. H. Whittle	Walter Snyder
1919	C. H. Whittle	Walter Snyder
1920	C. H. Whittle	Walter Snyder

	President	Captain
1921	C. H. Whittle	Walter Snyder
1922	C. H. Whittle	Walter Snyder
1923	C. H. Whittle	J. Burnett
1924	C. H. Whittle	Raymond Sentz
1925	C. H. Whittle	Raymond Sentz
1926	C. H. Whittle	Raymond Sentz
1927	Enoch Channey	Walter Snyder
1928	Enoch Channey	Walter Snyder
1929	George Arnold	Norman Fritz, Sr.
1930	George Arnold	Norman Fritz, Sr.
1931	George Arnold	Norman Fritz, Sr.
1932	John O. Cockey	Norman Fritz, Sr.
1933	John O. Cockey	Norman Fritz, Sr.
1934	John O. Cockey	Norman Fritz, Sr.
1935	J. Edward Hewes	Norman Fritz, Sr.
	George Fritz	
1936	George Fritz	Norman Fritz, Sr.
1937	Walter Harris	Donald Krauch
1938	Walter Harris	Donald Krauch

	President	Captain
1939	Walter Harris	Donald Krauch
1940	Lester Wheeler	Carroll Brown
1941	Lester Wheeler	Walter Harris
1942	Lester Wheeler	Walter Harris
1943	Lester Wheeler	Walter Harris
1944	Lester Wheeler	Walter Harris
1945	Lester Wheeler	Walter Harris
1946	Vernon Abbott	Walter Harris
1947	Harry Penn	Walter Harris
1948	George Fritz	J. E. Warner, Sr.
1949	George Fritz	J. E. Warner, Sr.
1950	George Fritz	J. E. Warner, Sr.
1951	Paul Boller, Sr.	J. E. Warner, Sr.
1952	Paul Boller, Sr.	J. E. Warner, Sr.
1953	Paul Boller, Sr.	J. E. Warner, Sr.
1954	Paul Boller, Sr.	J. E. Warner, Sr.
1955	Lawrence W. Reter	J. E. Warner, Jr.
1956	Lawrence W. Reter	J. E. Warner, Jr.
1957	Lawrence W. Reter	J. E. Warner, Jr.
1958	James W. Beck	J. E. Warner, Jr.
1959	Calvin Reter	J. E. Warner, Jr.

	President	Chief
1960	Calvin Reter	J. E. Warner, Jr.
1961	Calvin Reter	J. E. Warner, Jr.
	J. E. Warner, Sr.	
1962	J. E. Warner, Sr.	J. E. Warner, Jr.
1963	C. L. Wolfgang	J. E. Warner, Jr.
1964	C. L. Wolfgang	J. E. Warner, Jr.
1965	C. L. Wolfgang	J. E. Warner, Jr.
1966	R. C. Merriken, Sr.	J. E. Warner, Jr.
1967	R. C. Merriken, Sr.	J. E. Warner, Jr.
1968	C. L. Wolfgang	J. E. Warner, Jr.
1969	R. C. Merriken, Sr.	J. E. Warner, Jr.
1970	E. R. Brown, Sr.	J. E. Warner, Jr.
1971	E. R. Brown, Sr.	J. E. Warner, Jr.
1972	C. E. Cole	J. E. Warner, Jr.
1973	E. R. Brown, Sr.	J. E. Warner, Jr.

	President	Chief
1974	E. R. Brown, Sr.	J. E. Warner, Jr.
1975	Raymond Warner	J. E. Warner, Jr.
1976	Raymond Warner	Jere Whiteside
1977	Raymond Warner	J. E. Warner, Jr.
1978	Richard Cole	J. E. Warner, Jr.
1979	R. C. Merriken, Sr.	R. W. Stem, Jr.
1980	R. W. Stem, Sr.	R. W. Stem, Jr.
1981	R. W. Stem, Sr.	R. W. Stem, Jr.
1982	R. W. Stem, Sr.	R. W. Stem, Jr.
1983	R. W. Stem, Sr.	R. W. Stem, Jr.
1984	R. W. Stem, Sr.	R. W. Stem, Jr.
1985	Thomas Wolfenden	J. E. Warner, Jr.
1986	Calvin Reter	R. W. Stem, Jr.
1987	Calvin Reter	R. W. Stem, Jr.
1988	Edward C. Schultz	R. W. Stem, Jr.
1989	Edward C. Schultz	R. W. Stem, Jr.
1990	Edward C. Schultz	R. W. Stem, Jr.
1991	R. W. Stem, Sr.	R. W. Stem, Jr.
1992	R. W. Stem, Sr.	R. W. Stem, Jr.
1993	R. W. Stem, Jr.	Thomas Curtis
1994	R. W. Stem, Jr.	D. Wolfenden
1995	R. W. Stem, Jr.	D. Wolfenden Edward C. Schultz
1996	John Amole	R. W. Stem, Jr.
1997	John Amole	R. W. Stem, Jr.
1998	Paul Wilhelm	R. W. Stem, Jr.
1999	H. F. Renard	R. W. Stem, Jr.
2000	H. F. Renard	R. W. Stem, Jr.
2001	R. W. Stem, Jr.	Scott Warner

	President	Chief
2002	Edward C. Schultz	Scott Warner
2003	Edward C. Schultz	Scott Warner
2004	Edward C. Schultz	Scott Warner

County and State Officers

The Glyndon Volunteer Fire Department is a founding member of the Baltimore County Volunteer Firemen's Association. The Association was formed at a meeting held in Baltimore on September 20, 1907. The Glyndon Volunteer Fire Department is one of the original 14 member companies of the BCVFA.

Over the years, a number of the department's members have served as president of the association. They are:

1909	Harry W. Goodwin
1914	C. Howard Whittle
1929	George W. Arnold
1933	John O. Cockey
1949 – 1950	Walter Harris
1961 – 1962	C. LeRoy Wolfgang
1987 – 1989	H. Frank Renard

The department joined the Maryland State Firemen's Association in May of 1906. Mr. John O. Cockey is the only member of the department known to have served the MSFA in a leadership capacity. He was chairman of the Executive Committee in 1934 and served as a Trustee from 1942 to 1954.

Life Members (L to R) James E. Warner, Sr., Gorham Bowdre amd Kenneth Mosner.

Life Members of the Glyndon Volunteer Fire Department

George Arnold *
Carol Beimschla
Paul Boller, Sr.*
Gorham Bowdre *
J. Peter Brach, Jr.
Enoch E. Brown *
Earl R. Brown *
Clarence Caples
James E. Carter *
Carlton Chilcoat *
Henry S. "Tim" Clark
John O. Cockey *
Cornelius E. "Gene" Cole *
Richard Cole
James B. Eline
George Fritz, Sr. *
Norman Fritz, Sr. *
Elam Geist *
Blake Gore *
Vernon Gore
Walter Harris *
Charles Heflin *
Christian Heintzman
J. Edward Hewes *
L. Thomas Johnson
Russell Lessner
Mrs. Charles Lauterbach *
Fr. Joseph Lizor
Vernon Merkel
Mary Merriken
Richard C. Merriken, Sr.
Edwin L. "Buddy" Molesworth, Jr.
Edwin L. "Reds" Molesworth, Sr. *
Kenneth Mosner *
William Pearson, Jr.
Marvin Poe *
Calvin Reter
Edgar Rohde *
Dorothy Schultz
Edward "Ted" Schultz
Harry Shaffer *
Stewart Shaffer *
Joseph Simonds *
Richard Stem, Sr.
Richard Stem, Jr.
Rosemary Stem
Daniel Talbert *
Walter Talbert
Howard Turnbaugh *
Claude Warner *
James E. Warner, Sr. *
James E. Warner, Jr.
James E. Warner III
Raymond Warner *
Earl Welsh *
Lester Wheeler *
Jere Whiteside
Paul Wilhelm, Jr.
Doug Wolfenden
Tom Wolfenden *
C. LeRoy Wolfgang *

50-Year Members

George Arnold *
Casey Caples
John O. Cockey *
James B. Eline
Elam Geist *
Walter Harris *
J. Edward Hewes *
Kenneth Mosner *
William Pearson, Jr.
Calvin Reter
Edgar Rohde *
Richard W. Stem, Sr.
James E. Warner, Sr. *
James E. Warner, Jr.
Jere Whiteside

* *Deceased Member*

THE MEMBERS PAST AND PRESENT OF THE GLYNDON VOLUNTEER FIRE DEPARTMENT

A. Winfield Abbott

Anthony Altomonte

Harry Baker

Michael Baker

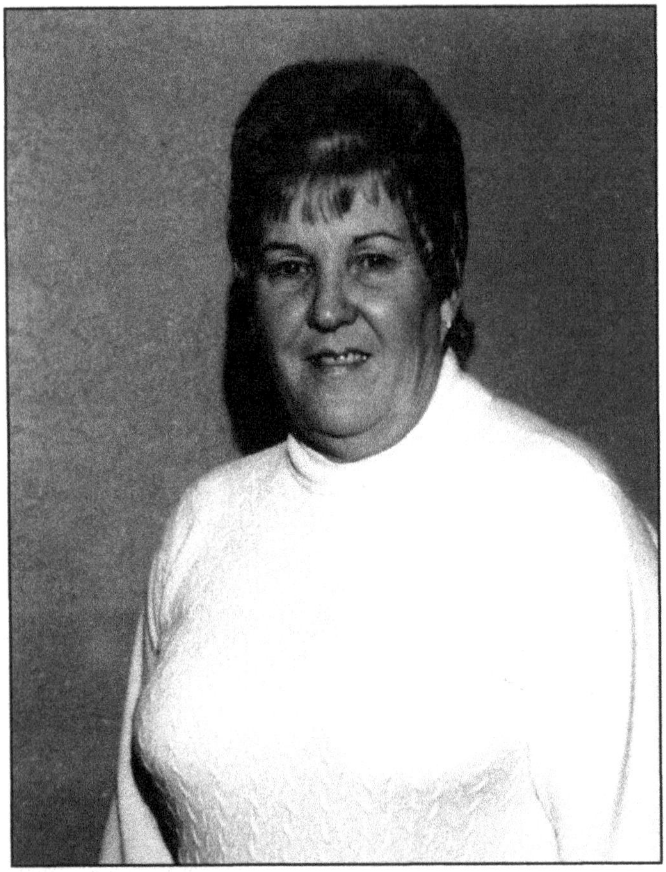

Carol Beimschla

Paul Boller (*)

J. Peter Brach, Jr.

Terry Brennan

Earl E. Brown (*)

Earl R. Brown (*)

Randy Brown

Casey Caples

Casie "Nickey" Carpini

Greg Carter

Jason Casey

George Clarke

C. E. "Gene" Cole (*)

Richard Cole

John Cox

J. Edward Crooks

Harry Curtis

Thomas Doyle

Daryl Ecker

James B. Eline

Ben Florie

Richard C. Fox

David Garnice

Marcia Garnice

Edward Goerdt

Vernon Gore

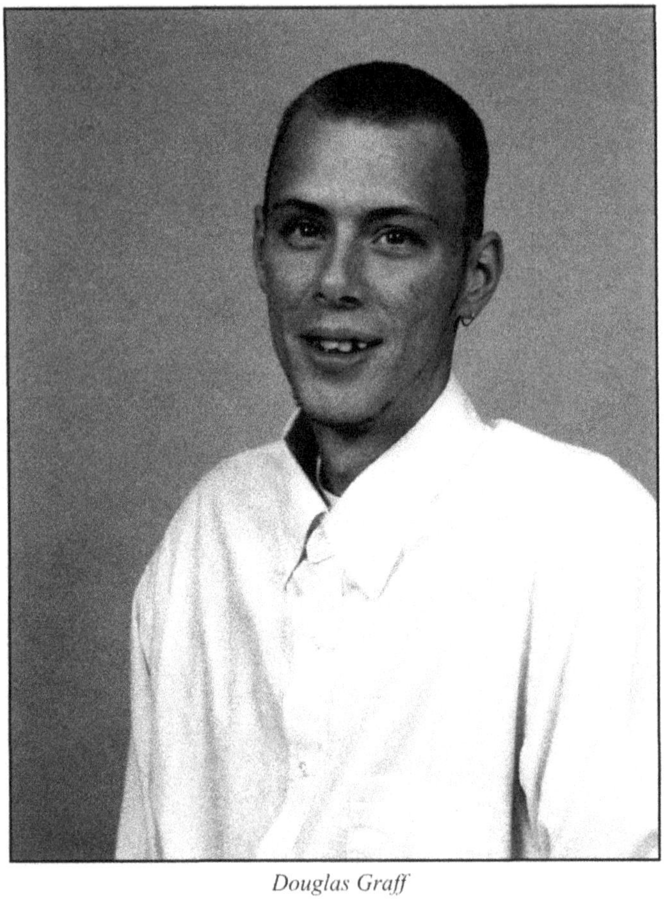

Douglas Graff

Walter Harris (*)

Charles Heflin (*)

Christian Heintzman

Donald Isennock

Robert Jackson

Thomas Johnson

Jill Warner Jones

David Knife

Russ Lessner

Matt Lewis

Marty Listwan

Father Joseph S. Lizor

Richard C. Merriken, Jr.

Randall C. Merriken

Russell C. Merriken (*)

Ronnie C. Merriken

Mary Merriken

Richard C. Merriken, Sr.

Michelle Mintz

Michael Mintz

Ronald Mintz

Edwin Molesworth

Donny Moorefield

Ken Morris

Thomas Moser

Pastor Norman Obenshain

William Pearson

Jamie Rarey

Kathy Reitz

Calvin Reter

John Rice

Mark Rome

H. Ben Rudow

Scott Rudow

Bruce Schultz

Dorothy Schultz

Edward "Ted" Schultz

Arnie Scher

Christina Staubs

Colin Stem

Rosemary Stem

Richard Stem, III

Richard Stem, Jr.

Richard Stem, Sr.

Walter Talbert, Jr.

Donna Warner

John Warner

Maxine E. Warner (*)

Maxine D. Warner

Mitchell Warner

Raymond Warner (*)

Scott Warner

James E. Warner, III

James E. Warner, Jr.

James E. Warner, Sr. (*)

Charles Webster

Monroe Wentz (*)

Jere Whiteside

Paul Wilhelm

Doug Wolfenden

Joan Wolfenden

Kathy Wolfenden

Scott Wolfenden

Thomas Wolfenden (*)

Louis Woodward

Rev. Edwin Wray

(*) Indicates Deceased Member

Photography by Bernard J. Roche

The Ladies Auxiliary

HISTORY OF THE LADIES AUXILIARY 1953 - 2004

Mrs. Frances Rook, Mrs. Rosemary Stem and Mrs. Susie Reter organized the Ladies Auxiliary of the Glyndon Volunteer Fire Department in 1953 for the purpose of helping the Glyndon Volunteer Fire Department. The first meeting of the newly formed auxiliary was held on March 10, 1953, in the old firehouse on Railroad Avenue. The first officers were Mrs. Frances Rook, President; Mrs. Susie Reter, Vice President; Mrs. Edward Wroe, Recording Secretary; Mrs. William Hammond, Corresponding Secretary; Mrs. Mary Lauterbach, Treasurer; Mrs. John Cockey, Chaplain; Mrs. Rosemary Stem, Guard. Mrs. Zulauf, President of the Baltimore County Auxiliary, installed the first officers. Mr. Paul Boller and the men of the department donated a new gavel and a check for $100.00 to help the ladies get started. There were ninety-four charter members.

The ladies immediately began what would prove to be an important role in supporting the work of the Glyndon Volunteer Fire Department. In May of 1954, the first fried chicken dinner was held. The first donation to the firemen was made in March of 1957 in the amount of $1,300, $1,000 for the building fund and $300.00 for the equipment. A pledge of $450.00 to the new Carroll County Hospital and a donation of $200.00 to the Maryland State Hospital Fund were also made. In 1959, a number of Buddy Dean record hops were held and they were a big hit.

When the new firehouse was opened in 1956, the ladies furnished the kitchen. The third anniversary celebration of the Auxiliary was held in the new building on Butler Road on March 13, 1956.

In March 1959 the men gave their first Appreciation Dinner and Dance for the people that had helped with the annual carnival. The affair also celebrated the anniversary of the department's founding in March of 1904. At the dinner, the ladies presented the firemen with two checks. They were in the amount of $2,500.00 for the building fund and $1,000 for the equipment. Each year since, the men have held a dinner and dance in March. The carnival is no longer held but the dinner and dance has been held each year to celebrate the anniversary of the department's founding.

In order to support the work of the department financially the Auxiliary served several public dinners each year on Sunday afternoons. They also catered luncheons, bowling banquets, dances, wedding receptions and private dinners. They held bake sales, a very successful one was held in 1959. A Sample Party held in 1963 and a visit by the ladies to the Harriet Andrews Research Lab in 1965 to sample different foods are indicative of the varied activities undertaken by the ladies in support of the men.

In 1974 Rosemary Stem and Maxine D. Warner joined the Glyndon Volunteer Fire Department and were trained as firefighters to help man the equipment during the day. Maxine E. Warner, Carol Beimschla, Mary Merriken, Donna Warner and Jill Warner joined them a short time later.

Over $75,000.00 has been donated to the Glyndon Volunteer Fire Department by the Ladies Auxiliary since they were organized in 1953. The Ladies Auxiliary donated the 1972 International Scout Brush Unit to the department. In March of 1979 the Auxiliary presented the men with a check for $10,000 as they celebrated their 75th anniversary. They also donated furniture for the new recreation room, curtains for the meeting room, recreation room and the hall.

The next 15 years were a very busy time for the Auxiliary with catering, banquets, weddings, private parties, public dinners, breakfasts and sub sales. Food was provided for craft shows, flea markets, open houses at the firehouse and casino nights. The Auxiliary supported the department's Monday night bingo with food service for 9 years, plus many other activities.

From 1980 through1993 the Auxiliary donated about $73,000.00 to the department. In addition the Auxiliary provided the department with a copy machine, computer and printer. They funded the renovation of the kitchen, a new dishwasher, new supplies for the kitchen and 200 chairs and new tables for the hall.

Three members of the auxiliary have served on The Baltimore County Ladies Auxiliary board and later as president of the county organization. They were Rosemary Stem 1981-82, Judi Stem 1991-92 and Joan Wolfenden 1997-98. Rosemary Stem is currently serving as Vice President for the year 2003 and will serve as President beginning in September of 2004. Marie Cole and Edith Linthicum are currently serving on the ways and means committee, and Joan Wolfenden is serving as color bearer.

"The Ladies Auxiliary is still active even though we are few in number" says President Rosemary Stem. "We have sub sales, bake sales, help with the public dinners and help with many of the activities held by the Glyndon Volunteer Fire Department. We proudly celebrated our 50th year of service in 2003."

Of the original 94 members, there are 8 members still active in the auxiliary, including LaRue Brown, Ruth Brown, Edith Linthicum, Mary Merriken, Rosemary Stem, Nancy Stocksdale, Maxine D. Warner and Mrs. Yates Wilson. Over the last 10 years we have lost 5 more of the original 94 members, Claudia Barnes, Susie Reter, Carrie Heflin, Ruth Warner and Mary Zentz.

The Ladies Auxiliary of the Glyndon Volunteer Fire Department considers it an honor and a privilege to have served the Glyndon Volunteer Fire Department for the past 51 years. We are dedicated to continuing our support of the department in their mission to provide emergency services to our community.

Officers of the Ladies Auxiliary

For the Year 2004

President – Rosemary Stem
1st Vice President – Marie Cole
2nd Vice president – Beverly Sikorski
Recording Secretary – Edith Linthicum
Corresponding Secretary – Jody Gore
Treasurer – Joan Wolfenden
Chaplain – Joan Wolfenden
Guard - Shirley Wilhelm

Janet Pfieffer, Past President, State Ladies Auxilary and Baltimore County Ladies Auxiliary introduces the officers of the Glyndon Ladies Auxiliary for the year 2004. (GVFD Photo)

Janet Pfieffer (Far Right) installs the officers of the ladies Auxiliary for the year 2004. (Photo by Bernard J. Roche)

Officers of the Ladies Auxiliary for the year 2004 (L to R) Rosemary Stem, President; Marie Cole, 1st Vice President; Beverly Sikorski, 2nd Vice President; Edith Linthicum, Recording Secretary; Jody Gore, Corresponding Secretary; Joan Wolfenden, Treasurer and Chaplain; Shirley Wilhelm, Guard. (Photo by Bernard J. Roche)

51 years of leadership
The Presidents of the Ladies Auxiliary
1953 – 2004

1953	Frances Rook	1979	Rosemary Stem
1954	Susie Reter	1980	Rosemary Stem
1955	Laura Rosendale	1981	Jody Gore
1956	Wiona Brown	1982	Jody Gore
1957	Wiona Brown	1983	Jody Gore
1958	Mary Sisson	1984	Jody Gore
1959	Laura Rosendale	1985	Jody Gore
1960	Lelia Otto	1986	Jody Gore
1961	Margaret Merkel	1987	Rosemary Stem
1962	Margaret Merkel	1988	Jody Gore
1963	Rosemary Stem	1989	Jody Gore
1964	Rosemary Stem	1990	Joan Wolfenden
1965	Wiona Brown	1991	Joan Wolfenden
1966	Margaret Merkel	1992	Joan Wolfenden
1967	Margaret Merkel	1993	Jody Gore
1968	Mary Merriken	1994	Jody Gore
1968	Elizabeth Fritz	1995	Jody Gore
1969	Elizabeth Fritz	1996	Jody Gore
1970	Elizabeth Fritz	1997	Jody Gore
1971	Elizabeth Fritz	1998	Jody Gore
1972	Rosemary Stem	1999	Jody Gore
1973	Maxine D. Warner	2000	Jody Gore
1974	Maxine D. Warner	2001	Jody Gore
1975	Carol Beimschla	2002	Jody Gore
1976	Carol Beimschla	2003	Rosemary Stem
1977	Maxine D. Warner	2004	Rosemary Stem
1978	Gladys Cole		

As The Glyndon Volunteer Fire Department, known to the dedicated ladies of the Auxiliary as "the men," celebrates its 100th anniversary it is appropriate that we express, as part of this history, our appreciation for the 51 years of support our "ladies" have given us. Support, which has made accomplishing our mission immeasurably easier.

MEMBERS PAST AND PRESENT OF THE LADIES AUXILIARY

Mae Allen (*) (++)

Peggy Baker (+)

Claudia Barnes (*)(++)

Carol Beimschla

Etta Mae Boller (*) (++)

Ruth Brown (+)

Marie Cole (+)

Beth O. Cooper (+)

Jody Gore (+)

Edith Boller Harnish (++)

Carrie Heflin (*) (++)

Irene Jackson (+)

Edith Linthicum (+)

Doris Hayes Long (*) (++)

Mary K. Merriken (+)

Gladys Pearce (+)

Susan Reter (*) (++)

Jackie Sainz (+)

Pablo Sainz (+)

Dorothy Schultz (+)

Eleanor Setzer (*) (++)

Beverly Sikorski (+)

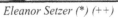

Judi Stem (+)

Rosemary Stem (+)

Richard W. Stem, Sr. (+)

Elizabeth Talbert (+)

Maxine E. Warner (*) (++)

Maxine D. Warner (+)

Ruth Warner (*) (++)

Shirley Wilhelm (+)

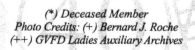

Joan Wolfenden (+)

(*) Deceased Member
Photo Credits: (+) Bernard J. Roche
(++) GVFD Ladies Auxiliary Archives

The "Sub Sale" (L to R) Shirley Wilhelm, Marie Cole, Claudia Barnes, Joan Wolfenden, Jody Gore. (Ladies Photo)

Preparations for the Ladies Auxiliary 50th Anniversary Party – 2003. (L to R) Joan Wolfenden, Shirley Wilhelm, Richard W. Stem, Sr., Jody Gore, Edith Linthicum. (Ladies Photo)

The Junior Fire Department

THE GLYNDON JUNIOR FIRE DEPARTMENT

THE GLYNDON JUNIORS

The Glyndon Junior Fire Department has had many faces over the years. The department's records first make reference to the "Glyndon Junior Fire Company" in 1912. At that time a junior fire company with at least seven members including Granville N. Baublitz, Robert Davis, George Bowers, Howard Arendt, Robert Martin, Fred Tome and J. Edward Hewes was sponsored by the Glyndon Volunteer Fire Company. A specific reference to the Junior Volunteer Fire Company is found in the minutes for November 18, 1915 describing an exhibition given by the juniors. References to the "junior fire company" are found in the department's records throughout the 1920s. There are, however, no detailed accounts of junior fire company organization or members from that era. The department did not attempt to organize a junior fire company again until the 1970s. The department's efforts to establish a "juniors" organization at that time were unsuccessful.

In April of 1993 the Board of Directors recommended proceeding with the organization of a Junior Fire Department. The department approved the recommendation on April 26, 1993 and the first applications were received on May 18, 1993. This effort to establish a junior's organization was, as the others that preceded it, short lived. Another effort to start a junior fire company was made in 1996. Dorothy Schultz and later Marty Listwan chaired the department advisors for this group that had at least 10 members.

"The Juniors" have been disbanded and reorganized a number of times but the overall concept of a junior fire department has remained the same, providing for the future of the Glyndon Volunteer Fire Department. There is an on going need for interested, dedicated and trained volunteers to fulfill the mission of the department to provide fire protection to the Glyndon community. The mission of the junior fire department is to nurture that interest in, and dedication to, the volunteer fire service at an early age. The program involves young people in the work of the fire service while providing appropriate training and youth oriented activities.

The most recent organization of a junior's program was begun in 1998 and was in the planning stages for four years. The research and planning needed for the current program proved to be a significant task requiring four years to complete. The Glyndon Junior Fire Department was officially reorganized in September of 2002 with four members, Richard Goldberg, Ryan Warner, Crystal Wilhelm and Scott Wolfenden. The group grew quickly to eight members and continues to grow with the membership approaching 20.

The Junior Fire Department is self-governed. The juniors elect their own officers and manage their own finances with the guidance of the senior advisors.

The group of advisors has also grown along with the juniors. In 2003 the junior department had a group of 6 senior advisors, Ken Morris, Mark Rome, Scott Rudow, Dorothy Schultz, Mitch Warner and Joan Wolfenden. These advisors are dedicated to the success of the junior's program.

Under the guidance of their advisors the members of the Junior Fire Department undertake projects and training geared to prepare them for membership in the Glyndon Volunteer Fire Department while having fun. The junior department is working on restoring a hand drawn hose cart owned by the department for use in parades, as well as helping to construct a "smoke house" as a fire prevention display. The members receive appropriate basic training in fire fighting techniques and participate in department training drills but do not perform tasks directly related to fire suppression.

The Constitution and By-Laws of the Glyndon Volunteer Fire Department allows members of the Junior Fire Department to apply for membership in the department at the age of 16. A number of members of the Junior Fire Department are planning to begin their required Firefighter I classes as they approach their 16th birthdays fulfilling the mission of the juniors program.

Glyndon Junior Fire Department Advisors 2004

T. Scott Wolfenden – Chairperson
David Garnice
Marcia Garnice
Ben Rudow
Dorothy Schultz
Joan Wolfenden

Glyndon Junior Fire Department Officers 2004

President – Colby Warner
Vice President – Courtney Garnice
Secretary – Ashley Brown
Ass't Secretary – Danielle Bolt
Treasurer – Ashley Wolfenden
Captain – Scott N. Wolfenden
Lieutenant – Ryan Warner

Officers of the Glyndon Junior Fire Department (L to R) Colby Warner, President; Courtney Garnice, Vice President; Danielle Bolt, Ass't Secretary; Ashley Wolfenden, Treasurer; Ryan Warner, Lieutenant; Scott N. Wolfenden, Captain; not pictured: Ashley Brown, Secretary. (Photo by Bernard J. Roche)

President Colby Warner introduces the officers of the Glyndon Junior Fire Department for the year 2004. (GVFD Photo)

Lee Sacks, 2nd Vice President Maryland State Firemen's Association (Far Right) Installs the officers of the Glyndon Junior Fire Department for the year 2004. (Photo by Bernard J. Roche)

MEMBERS OF THE GLYNDON JUNIOR FIRE DEPARTMENT 2004

Danielle Bolt

Ashley Brown

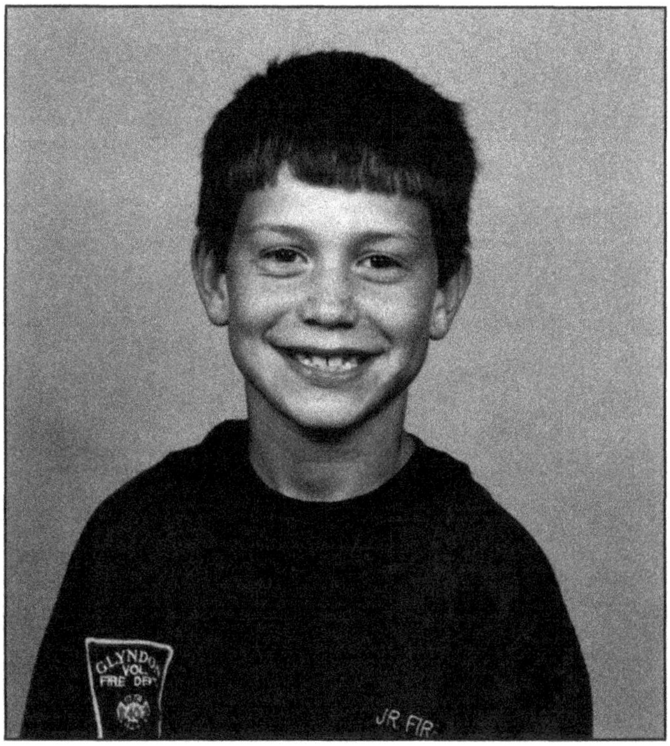

Bradley Fischer

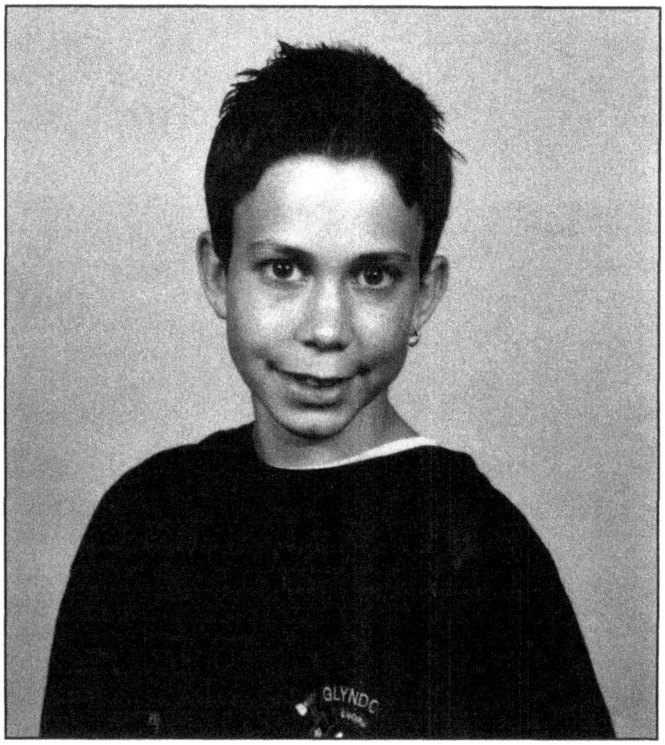

Robert Fischer

Courtney Garnice

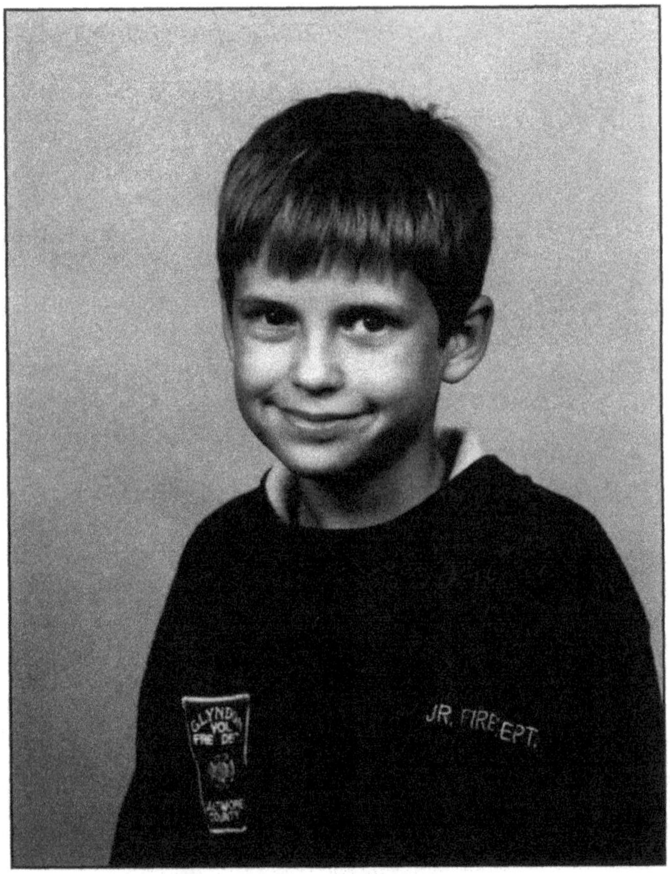

Vance Listwan

Kevin Ross

Matt Sikorski

Robert Smith

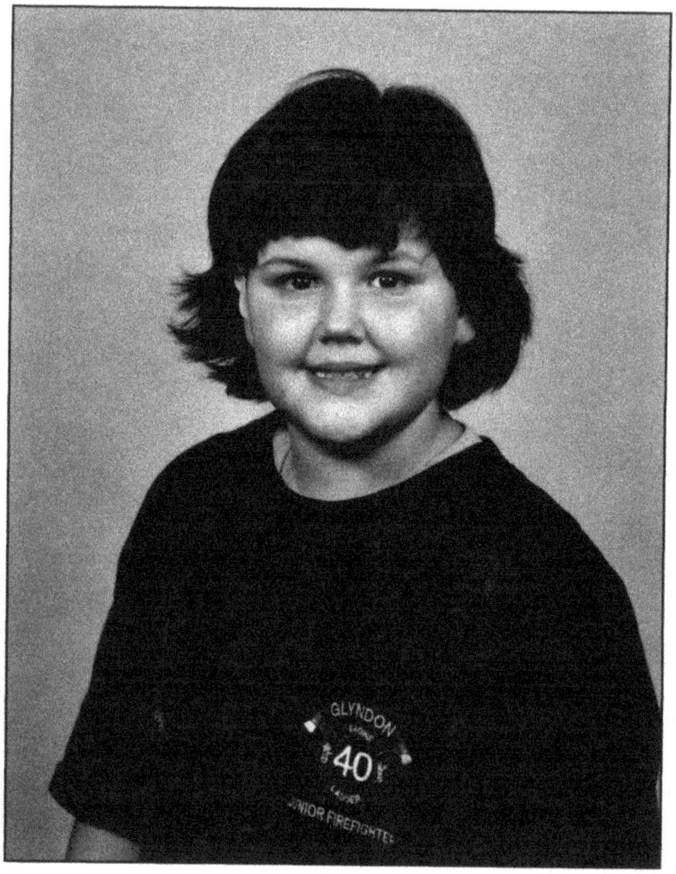

Amanda Staubs

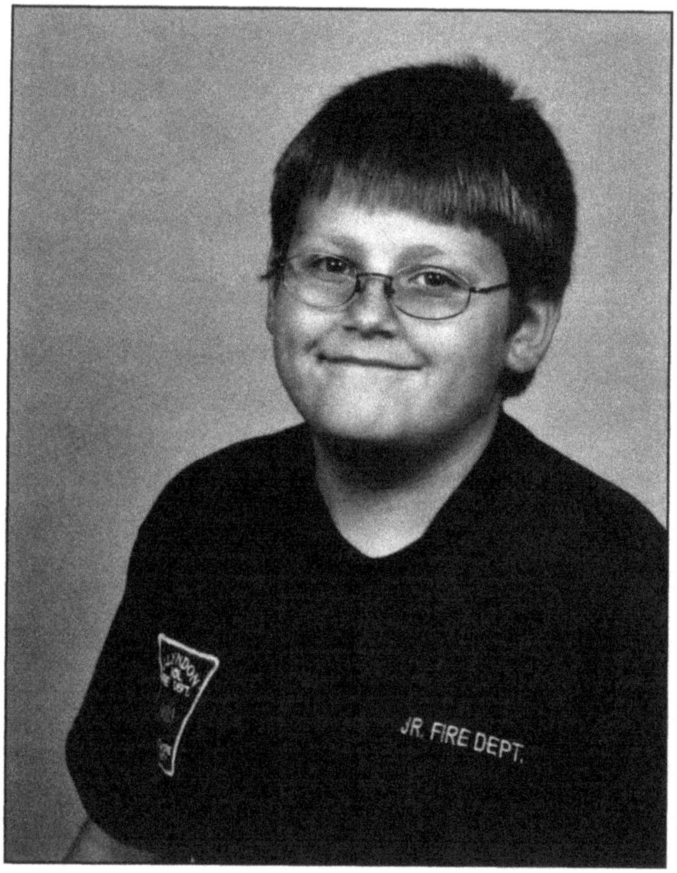

Colby Warner

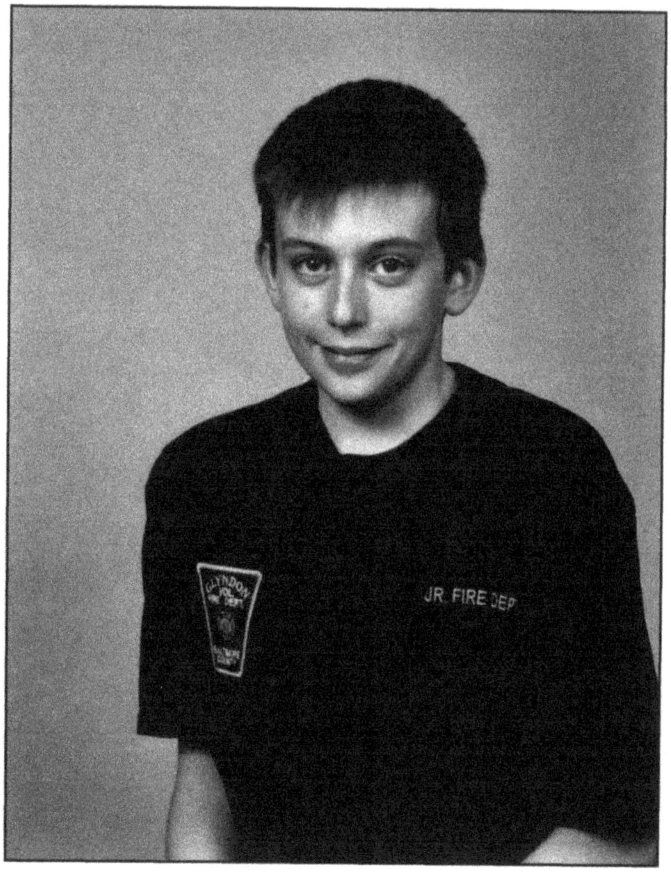

Ryan Warner

Crystal Wilhelm

Ashley Wolfenden

Scott Wolfenden

Photograph not available:

Samantha Himes
Cynthia McKean
Samantha Reitz
Nicholas Trott

Photos by Bernard J. Roche

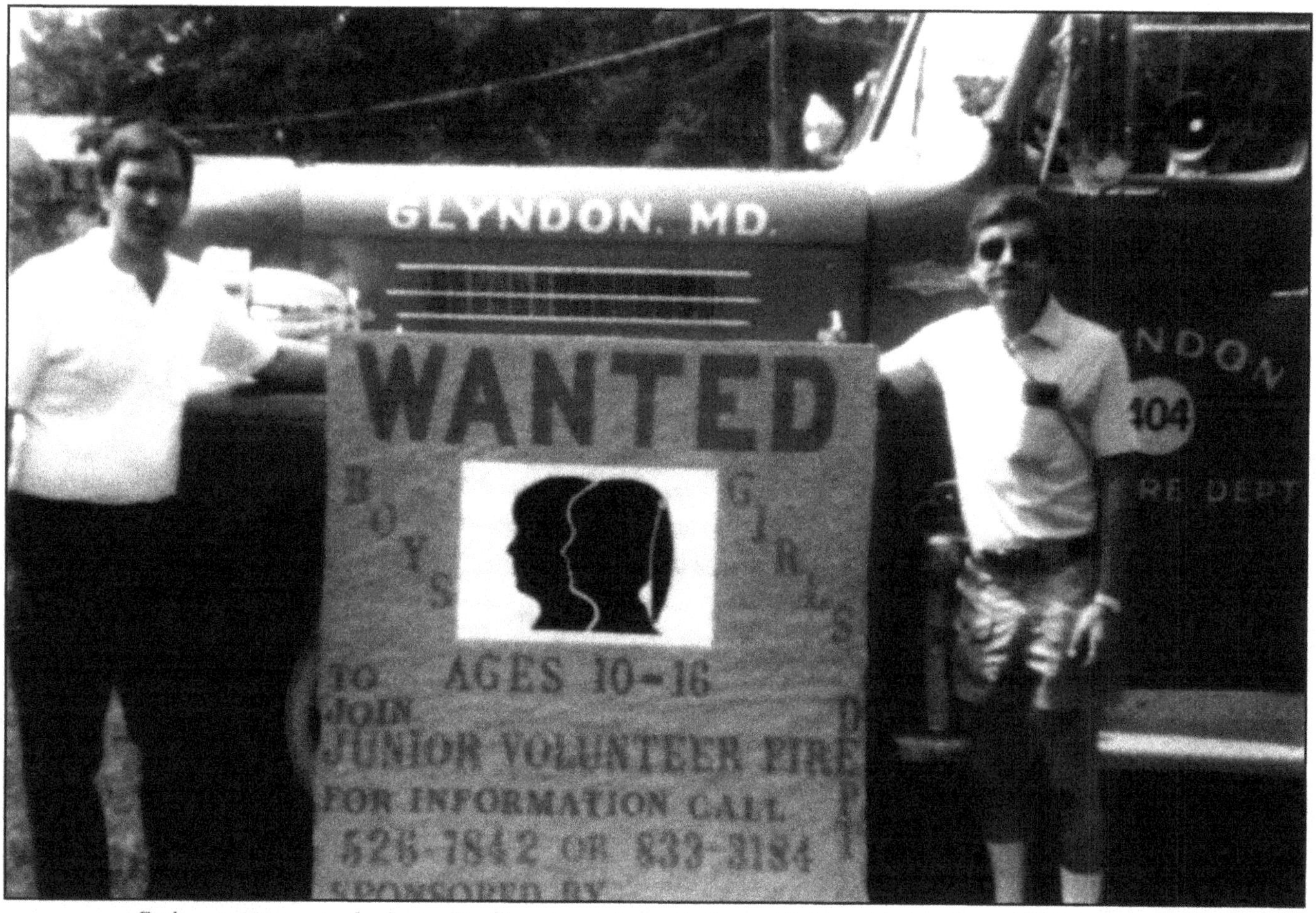

Early recruiting poster for Junior Fire Department. James E. Warner, III (L) and Arthur Clinton. (GVFD Archives)

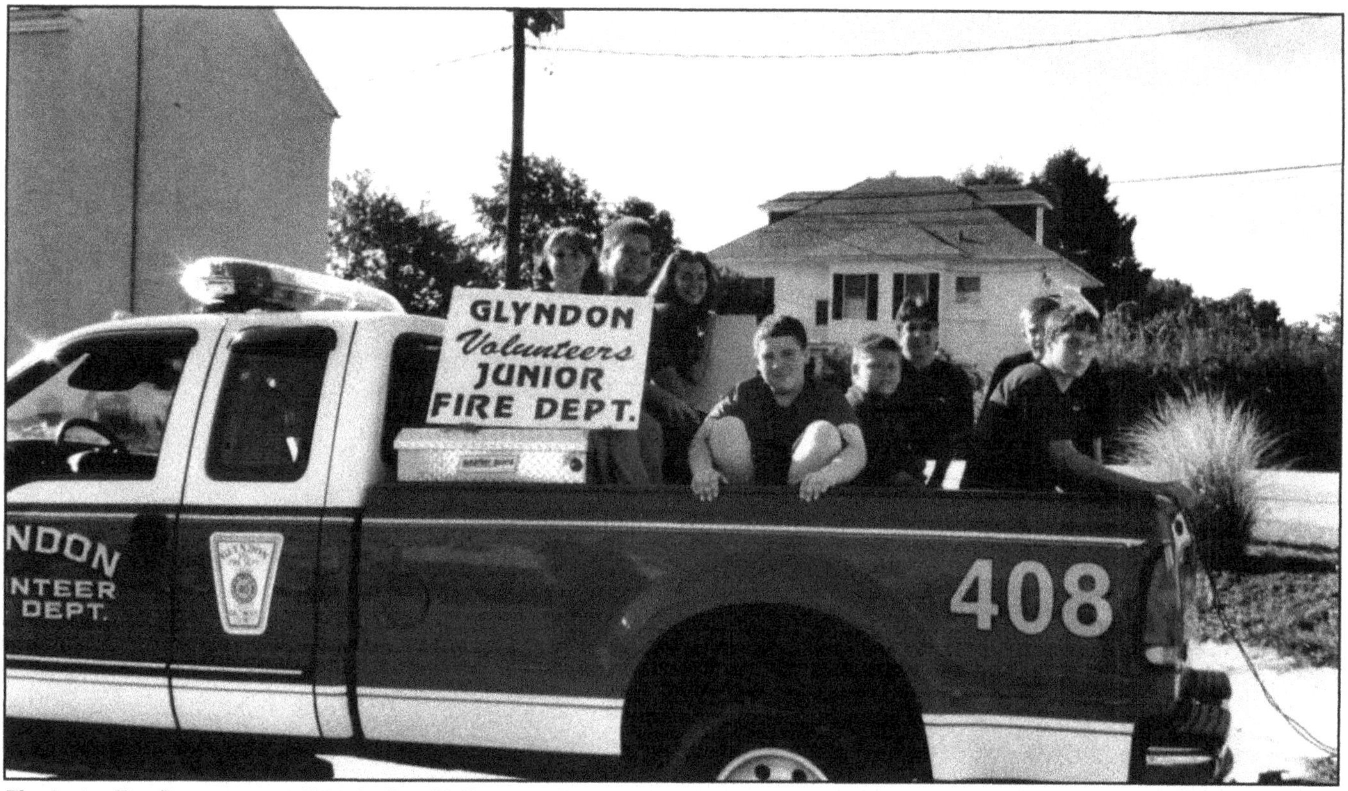

The Junior Fire Department on Parade (L to R) Courtney Garnice, Ben Rudow, Crystal Wilhelm, Robby Smith, Colby Warner, Marcia Garnice; Advisor, Ryan Warner, Scott Wolfenden. (Jr. FD Photo)

Celebrating 100 Years of Service
March 6, 2004

On March 6, 2004 two hundred and seventy-six members, friends and government leaders sat down to a banquet of traditional Maryland Crab Cakes and Filet Mignon to celebrate the Centennial of the Glyndon Volunteer Fire Department and fifty-first anniversary of the Ladies Auxiliary to the Glyndon Volunteer Fire Department. And a gala affair it was!

CENTENNIAL BANQUET
MARCH 6, 2004

Ladies Auxiliary Celebrating
51 Years of Service

Banquet Program

The Glyndon
Volunteer Fire Department, Inc.
cordially invites you and a guest
to attend our
100th Anniversary Banquet
March 6, 2004
Cocktails - 7:00pm   Dinner - 8:00pm
Wilhelm Ltd.
1011 Baltimore Boulevard
Westminster, Maryland

Welcome to the
Glyndon Volunteer
Fire Department's

100th Anniversary Banquet

MENU

Hors D'oeuvres

Cream of Crab Soup

Crab Cake and Filet Mignon

Gourmet Carrots

Confetti Roasted Potatoes

Cake and Ice Cream

Coffee and Tea

SOCIAL HOUR

INVOCATION — *Pastor Norman Obenshain*

DINNER

WELCOME & INTRODUCTION OF GUESTS — *Honorable James Malone*

GUEST SPEAKER — *Stephen Cox*

SPECIAL PRESENTATIONS

GOVERNOR — *Robert Ehrlich*

SENATOR — *Barbara Milkulski*

HOUSE OF REPRESENTATIVES — *C.A. "Dutch" Ruppersburger*

STATE SENATOR — *Paula Hollinger*

HOUSE OF DELEGATES — *Jon S. Cardin*

COUNTY EXECUTIVE — *Jim Smith*

COUNTY COUNCIL — *T. Bryan McIntire*

CHIEF OF THE FIRE DEPARTMENT — *John Hohman*

INTRODUCTION OF THE
GLYNDON VOLUNTEER FIRE DEPARTMENT ADMINISTRATIVE OFFICERS FOR 2004

PRESIDENTS AWARD
50 YEAR SERVICE AWARDS
LIFE MEMBER AWARDS

INTRODUCTION OF THE
GLYNDON VOLUNTEER FIRE DEPARTMENT BOARD OF DIRECTORS FOR 2004

INTRODUCTION OF THE
GLYNDON VOLUNTEER FIRE DEPARTMENT SUPPRESSION OFFICERS FOR 2004

TOP TEN RESPONDERS
TOP TEN TRAINING

CHIEFS AWARD
FIREFIGHTER OF THE YEAR AWARD
SPECIAL PRESENTATION - T. BRYAN McINTIRE

INTRODUCTION OF
THE OFFICERS OF THE LADIES AUXILIARY TO THE GLYNDON VOLUNTEER FIRE DEPARTMENT FOR 2004

INTRODUCTION OF THE
GLYNDON JUNIOR VOLUNTEER FIRE DEPARTMENT OFFICERS AND ADVISORS FOR 2004

BENEDICTION - FATHER JOSEPH LIZOR, JR.

2004 ADMINISTRATIVE OFFICERS

PRESIDENT — ***Edward (Ted) Schultz***

1st VICE PRESIDENT — ***Scott Rudow***

2nd VICE PRESIDENT — ***Kathy Wolfenden***

RECORDING SECRETARY — ***Dorothy Schultz***

CORRESPONDING SECRETARY — ***Kathy Reitz***

TREASURER — ***Richard W. Stem, Sr.***

ASSISTANT TREASURER — ***Frank Renard***

ASSISTANT CHAPLAIN — ***Joan Wolfenden***

CHAPLAIN — ***Pastor Norman Obenshain***

2004 BOARD OF DIRECTORS

Chairperson - ***James E. Warner, Jr.***

Justin McCracken
Scott Rudow
Edward (Ted) Schultz
Richard W. Stem, Sr.
Scott Warner
Doug Wolfenden

2004 SUPPRESSION OFFICERS

CHIEF — ***Scott Warner***

ASSISTANT CHIEF — ***Doug Wolfenden***

CAPTAIN — ***Randy Brown***

LIEUTENANTS — ***Justin McCracken***, ***Ronnie Mintz***, ***John Rice***, ***Chuck Webster***

2004 JUNIOR FIRE DEPARTMENT OFFICERS

PRESIDENT	*Colby Warner*
VICE PRESIDENT	*Courtney Garnice*
SECRETARY	*Ashley Brown*
TREASURER	*Ashley Wolfenden*
CAPTAIN	*Scott Wolfenden*
LIEUTENANT	*Ryan Warner*

2004 LADIES AUXILIARY OFFICERS

PRESIDENT	*Rosemary Stem*
1st VICE PRESIDENT	*Marie Cole*
2nd VICE PRESIDENT	*Beverly Sikorski*
SECRETARY	*Edith Linthicum*
CORRESPONDING SECRETARY	*Jody Gore*
TREASURER	*Joan Wolfenden*
CHAPLAIN	*Joan Wolfenden*
GUARD	*Shirley Wilhelm*

100th ANNIVERSARY COMMITTEE

Chairperson - J. Peter Brach
Jody Gore
Mary Merriken
Richard Merriken, Sr.
Kathy Reitz
Dorothy Schultz
Edward (Ted) Schultz
Richard W. Stem, Sr.
Rosemary Stem
James E. Warner, Jr.
Scott Warner
Joan Wolfenden

Past Members
*C. E. Cole **
Calvin Reter
Richard Stem, Jr.
*Thomas Wolfenden**
** - Deceased*

Brother When You Weep...

Brother when you weep for me
Remember that it was meant to be
Lay me down and when you leave
Remember I'll be at your sleeve
In every dark and choking hall
I'll be there as you slowly crawl
On every roof in driving snow
I'll hold your coat and you will know
In cellars hot with searing heat
At windows where a gate you meet
In closets where young children hide
You know I'll be there at your side
The house from which I now respond
Is overstaffed with heroes gone
Men who answered one last bell
Did the job and did it well
As firemen we understand
That death's a card dealt in our hand
A card we hope we never play
But one we hold there anyway
That card is something we ignore
As we crawl across a weakened floor
For we all know that we're the only prayer
For anyone that might be there
So remember as you wipe your tears
The joy I knew throughout the years
As I did the job I loved to do

Pastor Norman Obenshain (L) GVFD Chaplain delivered the Invocation.

Del. James Malone, Master of Ceremonies, kicks off the evenings the festivities.

Stephan Cox, the evening's guest speaker, delivered inspiring words to the assembled guests.

The Department is Honored by our National, State and Local leaders.

The Governor's Public Safety Liaison, Ken Zeigler, (R) presents citation from Governor Robert L. Ehrlich, Jr. to President Edward "Ted" Schultz (L) and Chief Scott Warner (Center).

Ms. Christine Botta presents citation from Congressman C. A. "Dutch" Ruppersberger. Accepting the citation on behalf of the Department are Chief Warner and President Schultz.

Ms. Julianna Albowicz, representing United States Senator Barbara Milkulski, presents a citation from the United States Senate.

Del. Jim Malone presents congratulatory message from United States Senator Paul Sarbanes to Chief Scott Warner (L) and President Ted Schultz.

Citation from the Maryland House of Delegates presented by Del. Jim Malone (L) Del. Dan Morhaim (Second from right) and Del. Jon Cardin (Far right). Greetings from the Maryland State Senate were presented on behalf of Senator Paula Hollinger

John Hohman (L), Chief of the Baltimore County Fire Department, presents a citation from Baltimore County Executive Jim Smith.

County Councilman T. Bryan McIntire (R) presents a citation from the Baltimore County Council.

Congratulations were received from the State and County Firemen's Associations.

Lee Sachs (R) 2nd Vice-President of the Maryland State Firemen's Association presents a congratulatory citation from the MSFA.

President, Joel McCrea (Far right) and Senior V. P. C. O. "Buddy" Staigerald, Jr. (Far Left) presents a citation from the Baltimore County Volunteer Firemen's Association.

Fellow Firefighters Honor the Department.

President Chris Burrows (L) and Chief Donald Isennock (Far right) of the Reisterstown Volunteer Fire Company Presents the Department with a commemorative bronze helmet.

Harry Wallet, President of the Owings Mills Volunteer Fire Company presents a plaque recognizing the 100th anniversary of the Glyndon Volunteer Fire Department.

Ms. Meredith Wells, representing Historic Glyndon Inc., presents scroll recognizing100 years of service to the community by the GVFD to Chief Scott Warner (L) and President Ted Schultz (R).

The Glyndon Volunteer Fire Department became the presenter when the Pikesville Volunteer Fire Company was presented with a plaque commemorating the company's rapid response to the Glyndon Depot fire on December 23, 1903. The loss of the Depot was a significant factor in the decision to form the Glyndon fire company.

Captain Samuel Dansicker (L) and President John Berryman (Second from Left) accept the plaque from President Ted Schultz and Chief Scott Warner.

Department Members are recognized for their Service.

Appropriately, the Centennial Banquet was the venue for the recognition of many of our members for service rendered to the department and milestones achieved during the year 2003. President Edward "Ted" Schultz and Chief Scott Warner presented the awards to the members being honored.

The Firefighter of the Year award for the year 2003 presented to Justin McCracken (Second from right) by Chief Scott Warner (R) with Assistant Chief Doug Wolfenden (L) and President Ted Schultz.

Councilman T. Bryan McIntire (R) presents citation from the Baltimore County Council recognizing James E. Warner, Jr. (Second from right) for his 61 years of service to the department. Chief Scott Warner and President Ted Schultz look on.

J. Peter Brach, Jr. (R) accepts President's Award for the year 2003 from President Ted Schultz.

Tim Clark (L) and Carol Beimschla (R) accept Life Member awards from President Ted Schultz (Second from right). Chief Scott Warner looks on.

Top Ten in Training Hours for the year 2003 (L to R) James E. Warner, Jr., Randy Brown, Tony Altomonte, Chuck Webster, Daryl Ecker, Edward Goerdt, Winn Abbott, Ben Rudow, Mitchell Warner, Scott Warner.

Top Ten Responders for the year 2003 (L to R) Ted Schultz, Dave Knife, John Rice, James E. Warner, Jr., Winn Abbott, Justin McCracken, Dorothy Schultz, Doug Wolfenden, Ben Rudow, Scott Warner.

President Ted Schultz (R) recognizes new 50-year members James B. Eline (L) and Casey Caples (Second from right). Jere Whiteside was also honored but was unable to attend.

Winfield Abbott (Center) accepts a Chiefs Award for the year 2003 from Chief Scott Warner with President Ted Schultz looking on.

Assistant Chief Doug Wolfenden accepts a Chiefs Award for the year 2003 from Chief Scott Warner with President Ted Schultz looking on.

The First Junior Fire Department Firefighter of the Year Award is presented to Vance Listwan (Front). Rear (L to R) Colby Warner, Scott Wolfenden, Ryan Warner.

The 100th anniversary committee accepts kudos: (L to R) Chairman J. Peter Brach, Jr., Rosemary Stem (partially hidden), Richard W. Stem, Sr., Joan Wolfenden, James E. Warner, Jr., Ted Schultz, Dorothy Schultz, Scott Warner, Kathy Reitz, Richard Merriken, Sr., Norma Brach and Mary Merriken. Not in Photograph: Jody Gore.

J. Peter Brach, Jr., chairman, 100th Anniversary Committee with past President and 100th Anniversary Committee chairman Richard W. Stem, Jr.

We had birthday Cake......
(GVFD Photo)

Lots of Birthday Cake!!!!!
(GVFD Photo)

Father Joseph Lizor, Past Chaplain of the Glyndon Volunteer Fire Department delivers the Benediction closing the evening's festivities.

Note: All photographs by Creative Imaging unless otherwise noted.

Fireman's Prayer

When I am called to duty, God
Wherever Flames may rage
Give me strength to save some life
Whatever be its age
Help me embrace a little child
Before it is too late
Or save and older person from
The horror of that fate
Enable me to be alert and
Hear the weakest shout
And quickly and efficiently
To put the fire out
I want to fill my calling and
To give the best in me
To guard my every neighbor
And protect their property
And if according to your will
I have to loose my life
Please bless with your protecting hand
My children and my wife

IN MEMORIAM

On March 5, 2004 the members of the Glyndon Volunteer Fire Department, the Ladies Auxiliary, joined by many friends and neighbors from the Glyndon community met at the Glyndon United Methodist Church to remember their deceased members. Guided by Pastor Norman Obenshain Chaplain to the Glyndon Volunteer Fire Department and Joan Wolfenden Chaplain to the Ladies Auxiliary we gathered to remember those that have completed their service here on earth and have received their reward.

The traditional Boots, Coat and Helmet honor our deceased members. (GVFD Photo)

We prayed together for Gods help and protection as we continue to selflessly follow the path we have chosen in helping others:

Almighty God, you rule all the peoples of the earth. In your sight, nations and peoples rise and fall, or pass through times of peril. Give us your light and truth. Lead the leaders of our nation by your wisdom; let honor and integrity guide their way. Help us walk through Life trusting you.

Merciful God, your goodness and protection keep us from harm. You inspire the mind and provide the strength for heroic men and women who guard this land as firefighters and paramedics.

Great God of strength and power, guard the brave men and women we honor this day. Thank you for all who have served this community and this country in the past with compassion and courage. Your shield of honor and faith goes forth with our men and women of the fire and medical services.

Generous God, thank you for all who have stood in the dim shadows of the background faithfully supporting the work of our emergency services, whose hard work and heartfelt prayers empowered those who answered each call.

Victorious God, teach us all to be soldiers of caring, men and women of God who uphold the truth, honor and dignity of others as we seek to serve you. Amen.

Walter Boyd, Vice Chaplain of the Baltimore County Volunteer Firemen's Association reminded us of "Gods promise of enduring care through trials and tragedies, floods and fire."

The Rev. Pete Roark, Pastor Emeritus of the Glyndon United Methodist Church and past Chaplain of the Glyndon Volunteer Fire Department inspired us with the story of how the prophet Elisha responds to a medical emergency and, by the grace of God a life is saved.

Pastor Obenshain delivered the message "In Gods Service" a reminder that we are not alone in our work and an inspiration to continue to serve. The text of his Sermon follows.

"In God's Service"

(Text: Isaiah 43:1-7, II Kings 4:18-37)

In the Biblical story The Rev. Pete Roark shared with us, a child died, of what sounds like heat stroke, or was thought to be dead and a mother was in anquish. This child was regarded as a special gift, as all children should be, from God. The prophet Elisha had arranged this with God out of gratitude for this woman's generosity. So, the loss was doubly grievous!

So she reached out to the one person she thought could help, the one who she connected with this child's birth, Elisha the prophet. Out of her extreme need she was insistent, and Elisha came. He did some strange things and the child revived. This Biblical story has its own design and purpose but it could be construed as a primitive description of mouth-to-mouth resuscitation. Whatever we say about it, by God's grace, a life was saved that day.

The work of EMTs and firefighters today is no less life-saving. We speak in religious circles of SALVATION and we attach certain meanings to that term, but at its root it means simply RESCUE. Firefighters and EMTs, in a basic way, are in the salvation business—saving lives and property and rescuing the stranded.

So, we are gathered here this evening to remember and to honor those who have faithfully served this community over the past century through the Glyndon Volunteer Fire Company. On an occasion like this certain themes present themselves for our thoughtful consideration: Memory, Service & Hope.

I. MEMORY is the gift of God that allows us to recall what is past, what has gone by. In this case we remember those who faithfully gave of their time, money and energy and, in one case, gave their life for the protection of Glyndon. Memory should lead, in this instance at least, to GRATITUDE. We thank those who have served Glyndon Volunteer Fire Company over the decades.

   It would be an ungrateful people, indeed, who did not appreciate what has been accomplished over the past 100 years. Even my brief reading of the histories of this area: Glyndon, Emory Grove and Reisterstown reveals what a scourge fire was to a Victorian village. A fire could rapidly sweep through the mostly frame construction of that day and easily trap souls inside. In a day when heat was often provided by some form of open flame and building codes did not yet require muliple exits, fire often led to death. Fire destroyed more than one hotel in Emory Grove, the tabernacle at the Chatauqua or Temperance Camp Meeting now known as Glyndon Park, and visited this site with devastating effect in December 1929 when the parsonage, sanctuary and Men's Bible Class all burned to the ground.

   We not only thank those who served, however. WE ALSO THANK GOD FOR THOSE WHO HAVE SERVED our community. We thank God for raising up volunteers and inspiring them to give their best.

II. That brings us to our second theme for this evening: SERVICE.

   A. I believe in firefighting parlance the term "in service" means that a company or an apparatus is ready to roll, that a pumper or tanker or company is in working order and has the necessary crew. We would rather have our equipment "in service" than "out of service," or out of commission, or out of order!

   B. The faithful service we celebrate tonight is part of building, and being in, COMMUNITY. The service of volunteers makes our communal life sweeter. It helps make the world more like how God created it to be!

   C. But SERVICE requires SACRIFICE. That sacrifice MAY be of life, but more often it is money, or time and talent. The hours spent at the firehall, or doing fundraising, or out on fire calls, or in the very extensive training now necessary to keep folks safe in our complex society—all those are hours that people could be doing OTHER things! It's a sacrifice to serve.

Whether we are connected with emergency services or not, however, WE ARE ALL CALLED TO SERVICE. We are all called to serve our fellow humanity. We are all called to be "IN GOD'S SERVICE." Those we memorialize tonight worked in God's service and we are called to do no less. May we be ever found in the SERVICE of our Saving God, our Divine King, our Creator.

III. We prayed earlier, "God, teach us all to be soldiers of caring." Emergency personnel are soldiers of HELP, who aid victims of natural and human created disasters. Therefore, they are soldiers of HOPE, which brings us to our final theme for tonight: HOPE.

A. The faithful work of those past should not only inspire in us a desire to serve but also should inspire hope in us, in our present day. The God who raised up volunteers in the past will continue to care for us.

B. Indeed, it is the over-arching love of God that makes human caring, compassion and commitment possible! Turning, for a moment, to our lesson from Isaiah, we find the promise of a God who cares. In this passage we find described a God who calls us by name and gathers together the stranded. Isaiah also has God say: When you pass through the waters, I will be with you; and through the rivers, they shall not overwhelm you; when you walk through fire you shall not be burned, and the flame shall not consume you.

Fire and water can be helpful to humankind, but they can also be two of our greatest enemies, fire and flood. These twins of wealth or destruction were certainly as known to the ancients as to us and this knowledge is reflected in the pages of the Bible.

It is not that we are necessarily SPARED from the disasters that visit this planet but we have HOPE because we know God cares. As the Shunemmite woman, in our second lesson, hurried, amidst her desperate grief, to saddle a donkey and run to see the prophet Elisha, she told her husband: "It will be all right."

Then, when she was met by Gehazi, Elisha's servant, inquiring as Elisha instructed, about why she came hurrying, she said: "It is all right." It IS all right. Even in her distress she could say it was all right. Even in our distress we can say "It is all right...because God cares."

We are called to trust in God, to trust in God's loving, protective care. For it is that divine care that ultimately inspires our HOPE.

So, tonight, as we celebrate the faithfulness of the past, may the MEMORY of their SERVICE played out in the presence of God inspire our SERVICE and our HOPE in the presence of God. Amen.

Pastor Norman Obenshain
Glyndon United Methodist Church
Chaplain, GVFD

The deceased members of the Department were honored with the ceremonial sounding of the Department's bell. The bell was sounded once for each 50 years of the Department's history.

Following a long-standing Fire Service tradition The Fire Brigade of Greater Baltimore Pipes and Drums led the procession of our members in to the church and led the recessional at the conclusion of the service. During the service the Pipers played a number of traditional hymns. We wish to thank them for joining us and contributing so much to our memorial service.

In the 100-year history of the Glyndon Volunteer Fire Department two of our members have made the ultimate sacrifice. One in the service of his community while engaged in fire fighting operations and the other in the service of his country on the battlefield of Vietnam. They served the community of Glyndon and their Nation with dedication and distinction. We are proud to honor them here.

In Memoriam
Raymond E. Otto

1917 - 1968
Otto Family Photo

On February 19, 1968 Raymond E. Otto suffered a fatal heart attack while engaged in firefighting operations. In the 100-year history of the Department he is the only member to die in the line of duty.

On the occasion of our 100th anniversary the Glyndon Volunteer Fire Department re-affirms the high regard in which we hold our fallen brother with this resolution, drawn first at the time of his death and repeated here, attesting to the great sense of loss and sadness his death brought to the Department, his family and the community.

RESOLUTION
OF THE
MEMBERS OF THE GLYNDON VOLUNTEER
FIRE DEPARTMENT, INC., OF BALTIMORE COUNTY
UPON THE DEATH OF THEIR MEMBER
RAYMOND E. OTTO

We, the members of the Glyndon Volunteer Fire Department, Inc. learned with sorrow of the death of our friend and fellow member, Raymond E. Otto, whom our Heavenly Father so suddenly called from a fruitful and active earthly life to his eternal home. Raymond was dedicated not only to the fire company, but to his home, family, friends and community. As an active member and officer of the Glyndon Volunteer Fire Department, Inc. for many years, he was courteous, capable and loyal in fulfilling the duties called for by his position.

We bear affectionate testimony to the consistency of his life and his recognition of the superior obligations placed upon him by his Christian life.

We desire to place on record this expression of our estimate of his life and work among us and to assure his wife and his family of our deep sympathy for them in this, their time of sorrow.

THEREFORE, BE IT RESOLVED, that this testimonial be placed among the records of the Glyndon Volunteer Fire Department, Inc. and that a copy thereof be sent to his wife, Lela G. Otto.

TEST:

Clarence W. Caples

GLYNDON VOLUNTEER FIRE DEPARTMENT, INC.

C. LeRoy Wolfgang
C. LeRoy Wolfgang, President

IN MEMORIAM

JAMES WILLIAM LEAF

1948 – 1969
U.S. Army Photo

On February 23, 1969 SP4 James William Leaf died as a result of enemy action while serving with the United States Army in Binh Duong Province, South Vietnam. Jim was elected to membership in the Glyndon Volunteer fire Department on April 25, 1966 and actively participated in Department activities until his induction into the United States Army in 1968. He continued as a member of the Department until his untimely death in 1969. James Leaf is the only member of the Department to have given his life in the service of his Country.

As we celebrate our 100th Anniversary we prayerfully recall the sacrifice that James Leaf made in the service of us all and celebrate his memory as an example of truly dedicated service to his Nation and his Community.

Do not forget me when my valley's hushed
And white with snow,
Grass growing green in the summer of my meadow
Help me see the peace I lived and died for grow.

Excerpt from A Combat Soldier's Prayer
Gary Jacobson

James W. Leaf is honored on The Wall: Panel 31W – Row 008

The Photo Album

ENGINE
40
LADDER

GVFD Memories

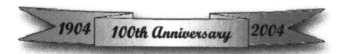

1904 100th Anniversary 2004

GVFD Photos

(L to R) George Randall, Lawrence Reter (seated on desk), unidentified member (hidden), James E. Warner, Jr., James E. Warner, Sr. and unidentified member (back to camera). (GVFD Archives)

Edwin "Reds" Molesworth, Sr. (GVFD Archives)

Training at Bay Shore Park. Buddy Molesworth carries dummy down ladder. (GVFD Archives)

1947 Mack engine at training exercise. (L to R) James E. Warner, Jr., unidentified, Edwin "Buddy" Molesworth Jr., Chief Winfield Weinholt (BCFD), LeRoy " Mickey" Wolfgang, unidentified, Bud Hammond (RVFC). (GVFD Archives)

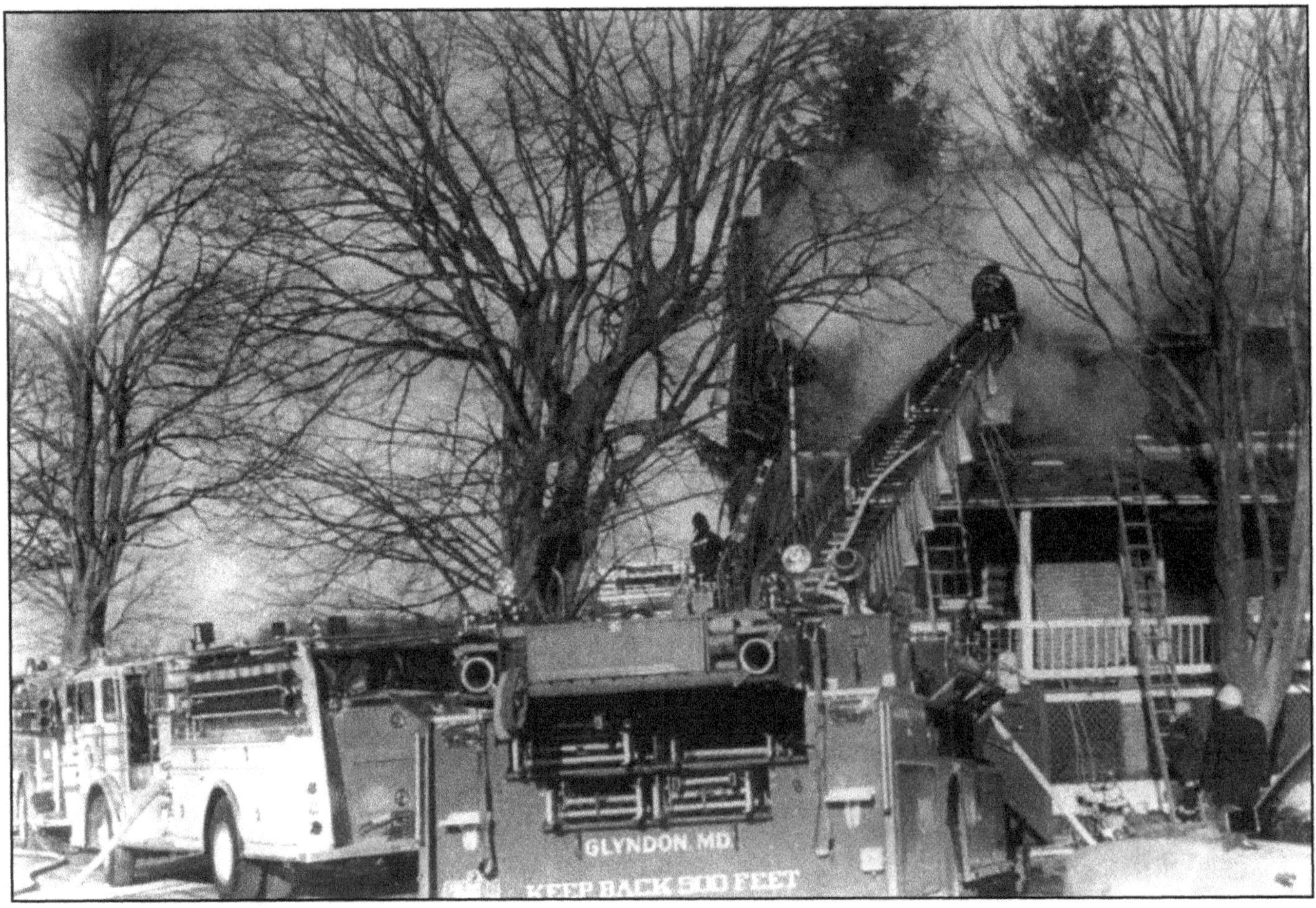

Fire – Manchester, Maryland, 1978. (GVFD Archives)

"Mickey" Wolfgang (L) and "Buddy" Molesworth training on the 1947 Mack engine. (GVFD Archives)

Pump Contest at Pikesville VFC September 21, 1957. (L to R) LeRoy Wolfgang (connecting to the hydrant), Casey Caples, Buddy Brunk, Gene Cole. (GVFD Archives)

Underwriter's Test of 1959 Mack engine, May 29, 1959. Front (L to R) Robert Klinefelter, C. E. "Gene" Cole, C. LeRoy "Mickey" Wolfgang, Jere Whiteside. Rear (L to R) Edwin "Reds" Molesworth, Chief Winfield Wineholt; BCFD, J. Himes, Underwriter's representative; James E. Warner, Jr., Bob Heusner, Mack Company representative. (GVFD Archives)

President Richard Stem, Sr. with Past President Richard Merriken, Sr. (GVFD Archives)

(L to R) Wiona Brown, Doris Long, Alma Whiteside, Lottie Molesworth, Laura Fritz. (Ladies Archives)

(L to R) Doris Long, Wiona Brown, Marty Cockey, Madeline Hoadley, Lottie Molesworth, Jean Reter, Laura Rosendale. (Ladies Archives)

(L to R) Ruth Brown, Wiona Brown, Sue Laudeman, Elizabeth Kuhleman, Elizabeth Talbert, Mary Merriken, Margaret Merkel, Lilia Otto. (Ladies Archives)

(L to R) Lilia Otto, Treva Keefer, Alma Whiteside, Margaret Merkel, Claudia Barnes and Ruth Brown. (Ladies Archives)

Mrs. Frances Rook, First President and Founding Member of the Ladies Auxiliary. (Ladies Archives)

Buddy Dean at a Record Hop, a popular fundraiser. (Ladies Archives)

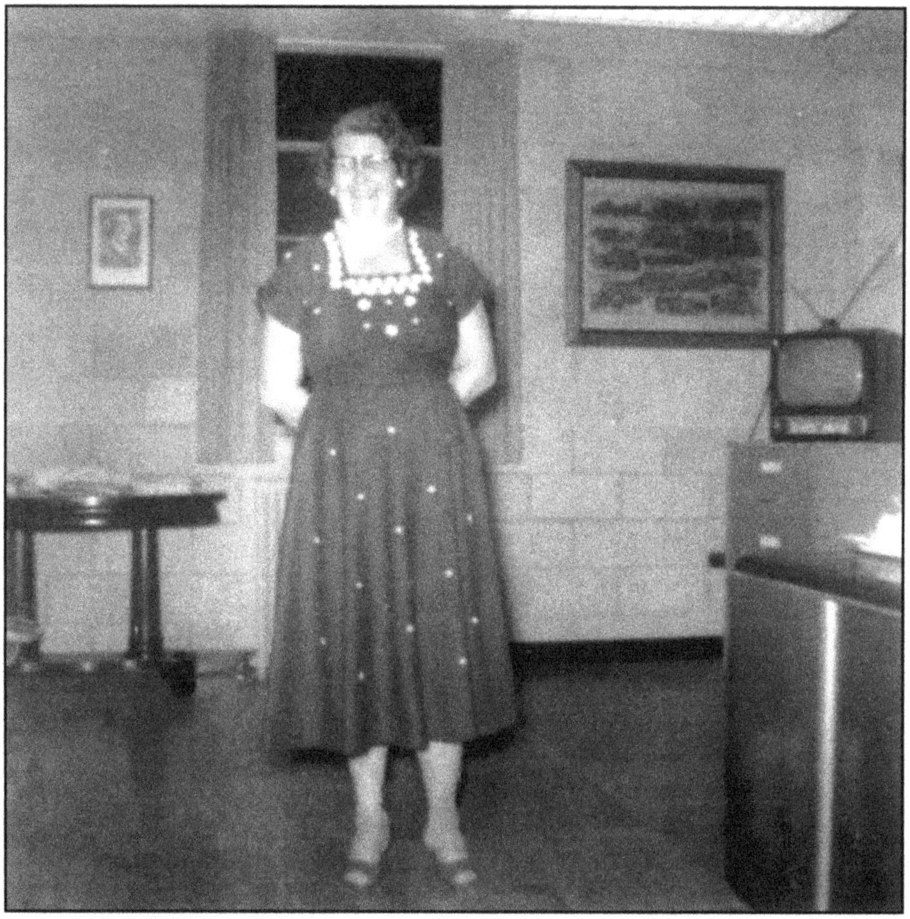

Susie Reter, Founding Member of the Ladies Auxiliary. (Ladies Archives)

Left: Rosemary Stem (founding member) and Joan Wolfenden at BCVFA Auxiliary meeting. (Ladies Photo)

"The really big one." Suburban Propane June 23, 1979, Boring, Maryland. (GVFD Photo)

Suburban Propane (GVFD Photo)

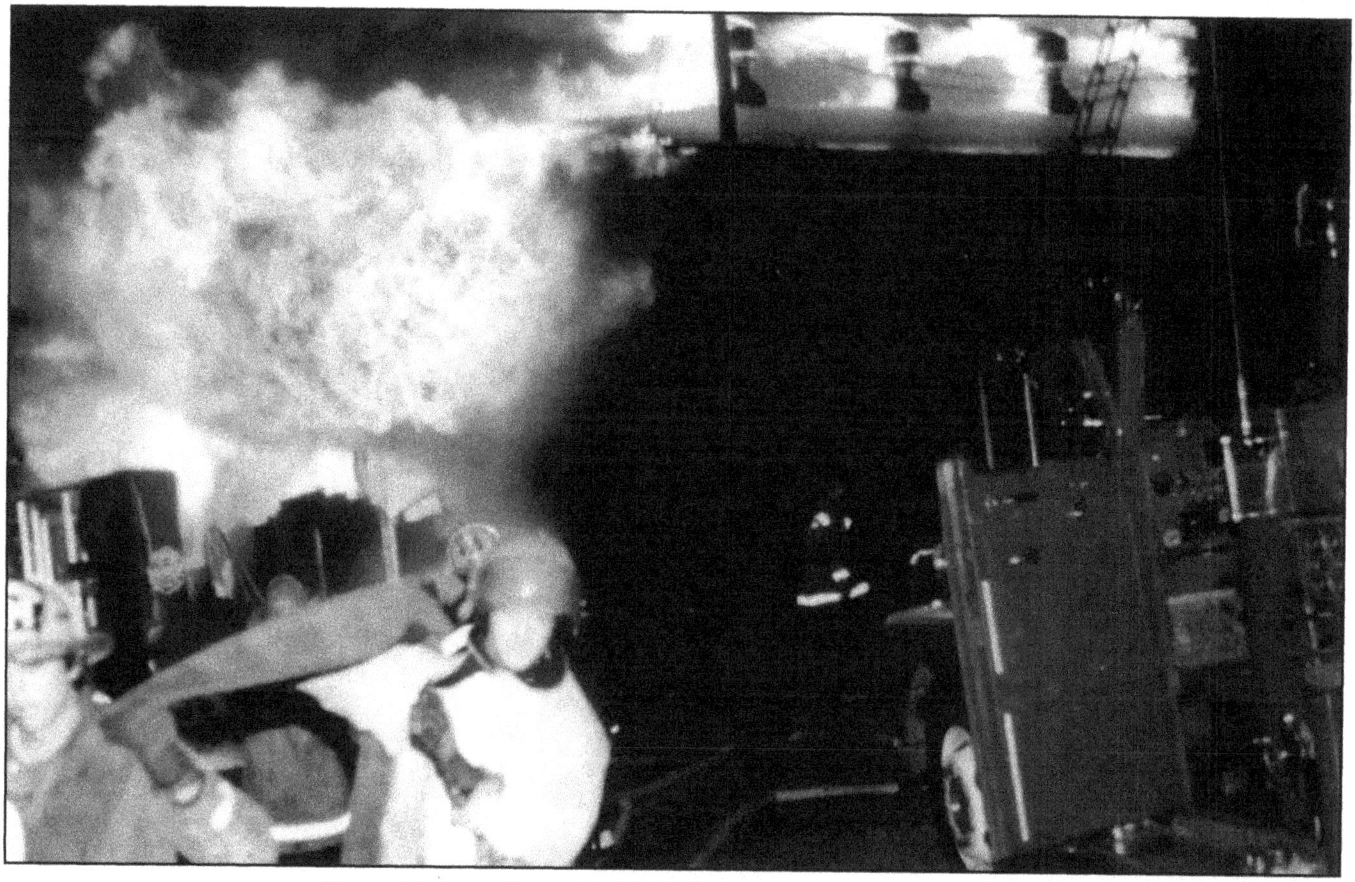

Fosters Mushroom Farm, July 15, 1980, Glyndon, Maryland. (VFD Photo)

Fosters Mushroom Farm (GVFD Photo)

Back: (L to R) Maxine D. Warner, Carrie Heflin, Nancy Stocksdale, Claudia Barnes, Rosemary Stem, Mary Merriken. Front: (L to R) Susie Reter, May Allen, Mary Larkins. (Ladies Archives)

Getting ready for the Spring Oyster Supper. (Ladies Photo)

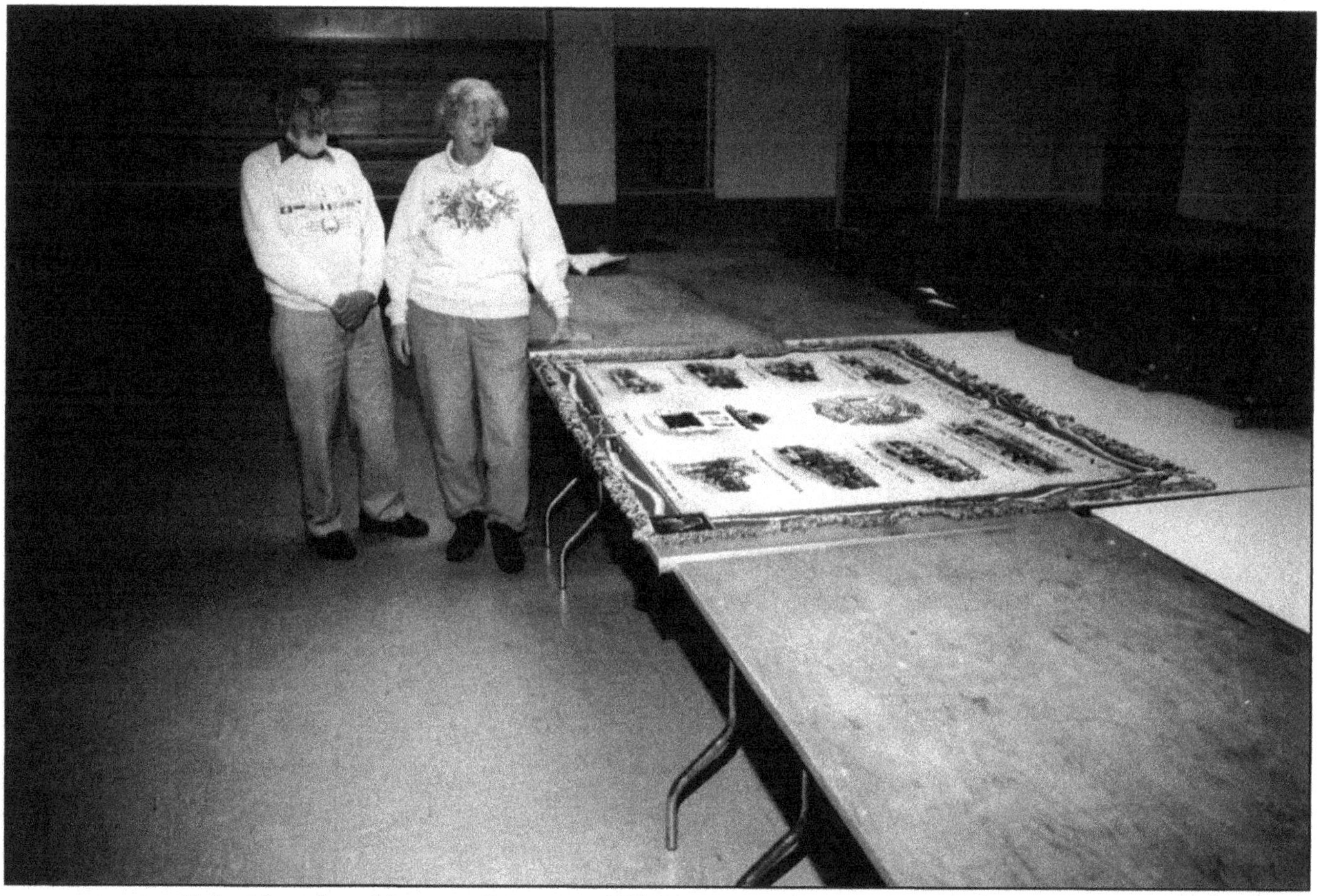

Richard Stem, Sr. and Rosemary Stem inspect 100th Anniversary commemorative Afghan. (GVFD Photo)

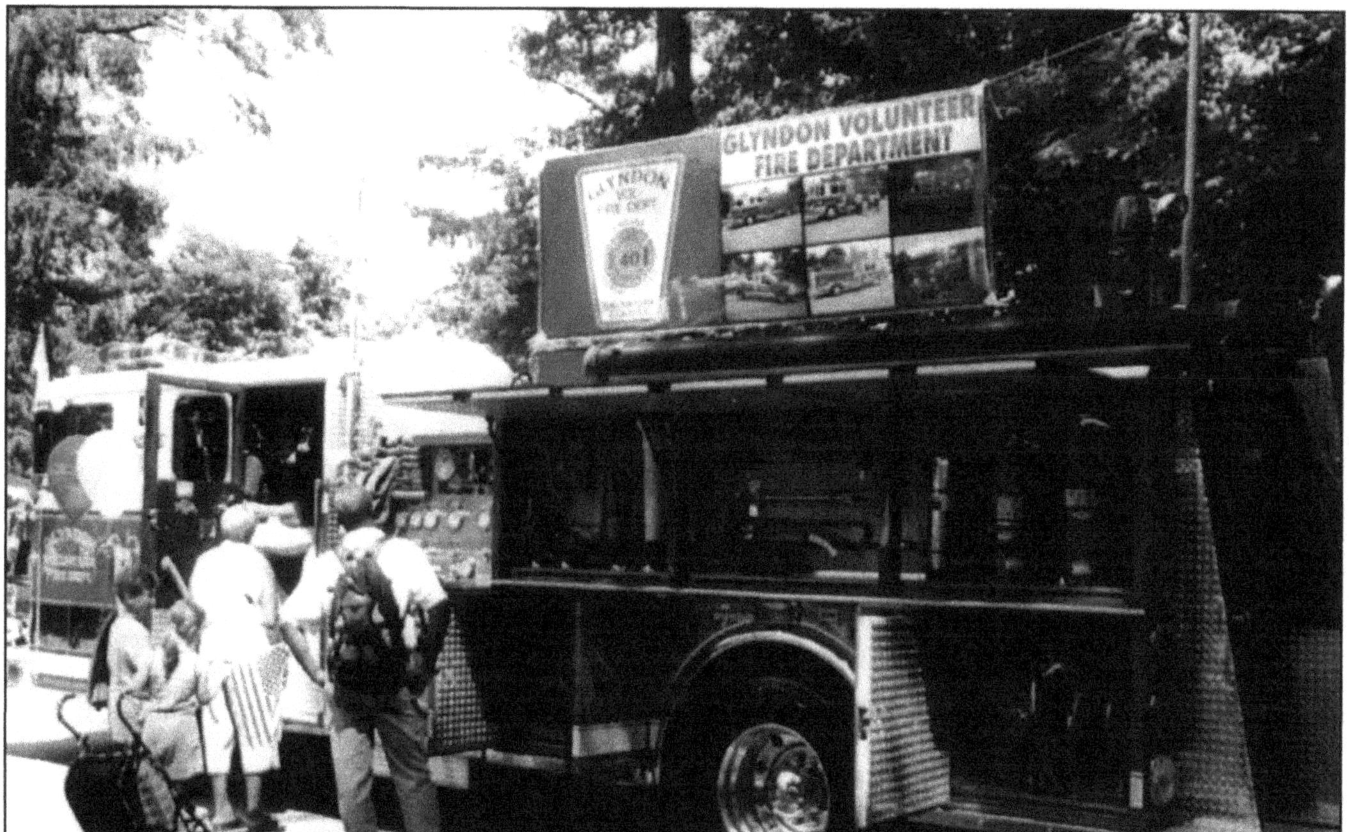

The Glyndon VFD display at the Reister's Towne Festival. (GVFD Photo)

Jere Whiteside dons proximity suit while Toby Carter (RFVC) watches. (GVFD Photo)

"This thing really works!" (GVFD Photo)

Members at dedication of Special Unit 407. Standing (L to R) Chief Scott Warner, Ben Rudow, John Vance, John Warner, Ed Goerdt, Dave Knife, Scott Rudow, Tony Altomonte, Dorothy Schultz, James E. Warner, Jr., Rick Cole, Marty Listwan, Doug Wolfenden, Kathy Wolfenden, Randy Brown. Seated (L to R) Chuck Webster, Paul Wilhelm, Winfield Abbott, Ben Florie. (GVFD Photo)

Members in front of the Fire House. Rear standing (L to R) John Rice, Edward "Ted" Schultz, Dorothy Schultz, Kenny Morris, James E. Warner, Jr., Dave Knife (wearing mask), Lieutenants Tony Altomonte, Jason Casey and Scott Rudow. Front kneeling (L to R) Kathy Wolfenden, Nikki Carpini, Captain Arne Scher, Chief Scott Warner, Assistant Chief Doug Wolfenden, Mitch Warner and Ben Rudow. (GVFD Photo)

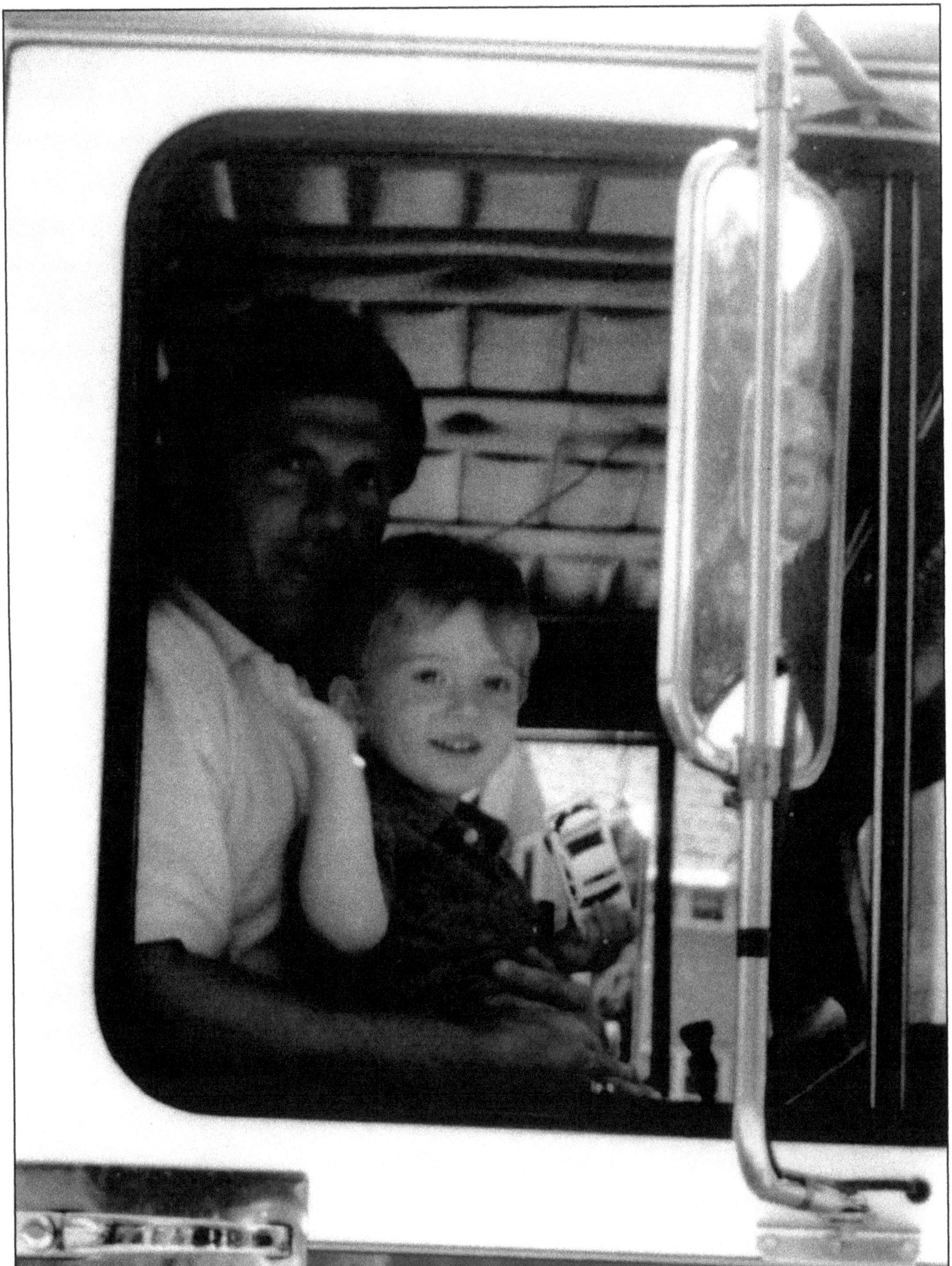

Maryland Governor Robert L. Ehrlich with son Drew at Birthday Party held at GVFD. (Photo provided by Governor Ehrlich)

Led by a Piper, the 100th Anniversary Parade moves down Railroad Avenue in Glyndon. The Junior Fire Department follows with the Department's hand drawn hose cart.

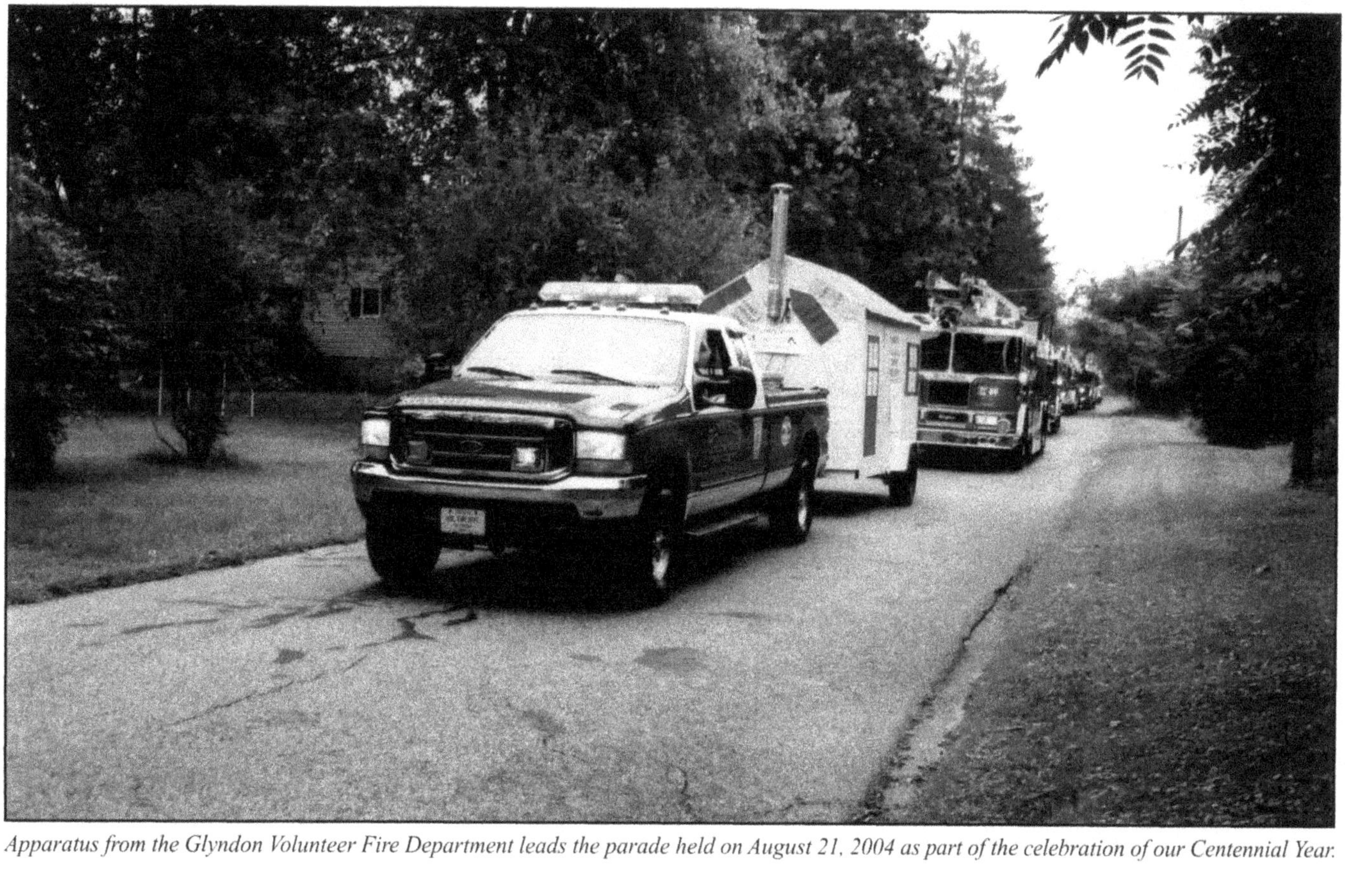

Apparatus from the Glyndon Volunteer Fire Department leads the parade held on August 21, 2004 as part of the celebration of our Centennial Year.

Members of the Junior Fire Department assemble for the Centennial Parade. (L to R) Courtney Garnice, Danielle Bolt, Kevin Ross, Advisor Joan Wolfenden, Nick Trott, Ryan Warner, Advisor Dorothy Schultz and Colby Warner. (GVFD Photo)

Sparky the Fire Dog joins the apparatus display at our Fire Prevention Open House, October 3, 2004. (GVFD Photo)

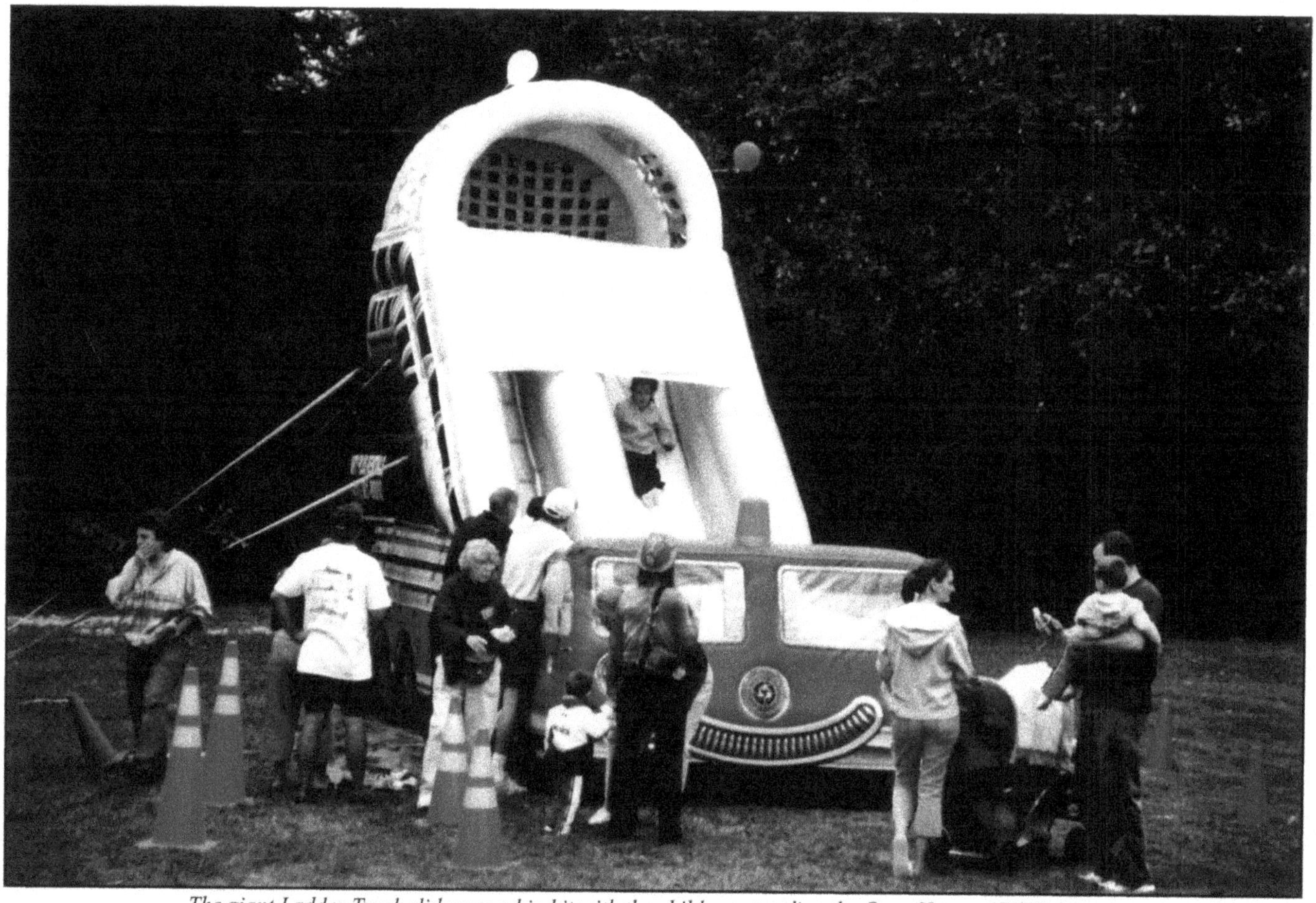

The giant Ladder Truck slide was a big hit with the children attending the Open House. (GVFD Photo)

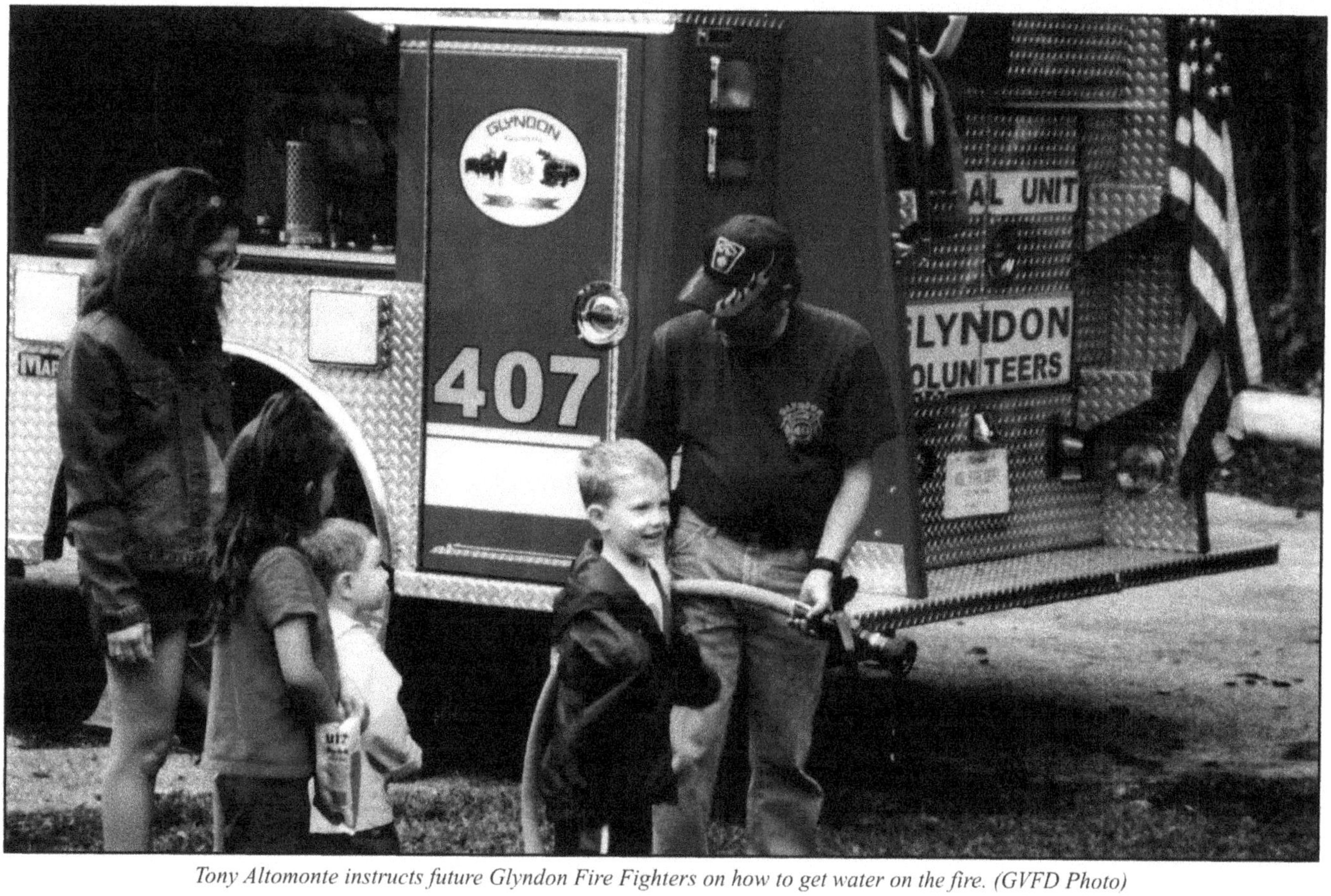

Tony Altomonte instructs future Glyndon Fire Fighters on how to get water on the fire. (GVFD Photo)

Sparky the Fire Dog greets children at the Fire Prevention Open House with a Fire Safety message. (GVFD Photo)

The B.C.V.F.A. Fire Safety House teaches children and adults alike important fire safety and survival skills. (GVFD Photo)

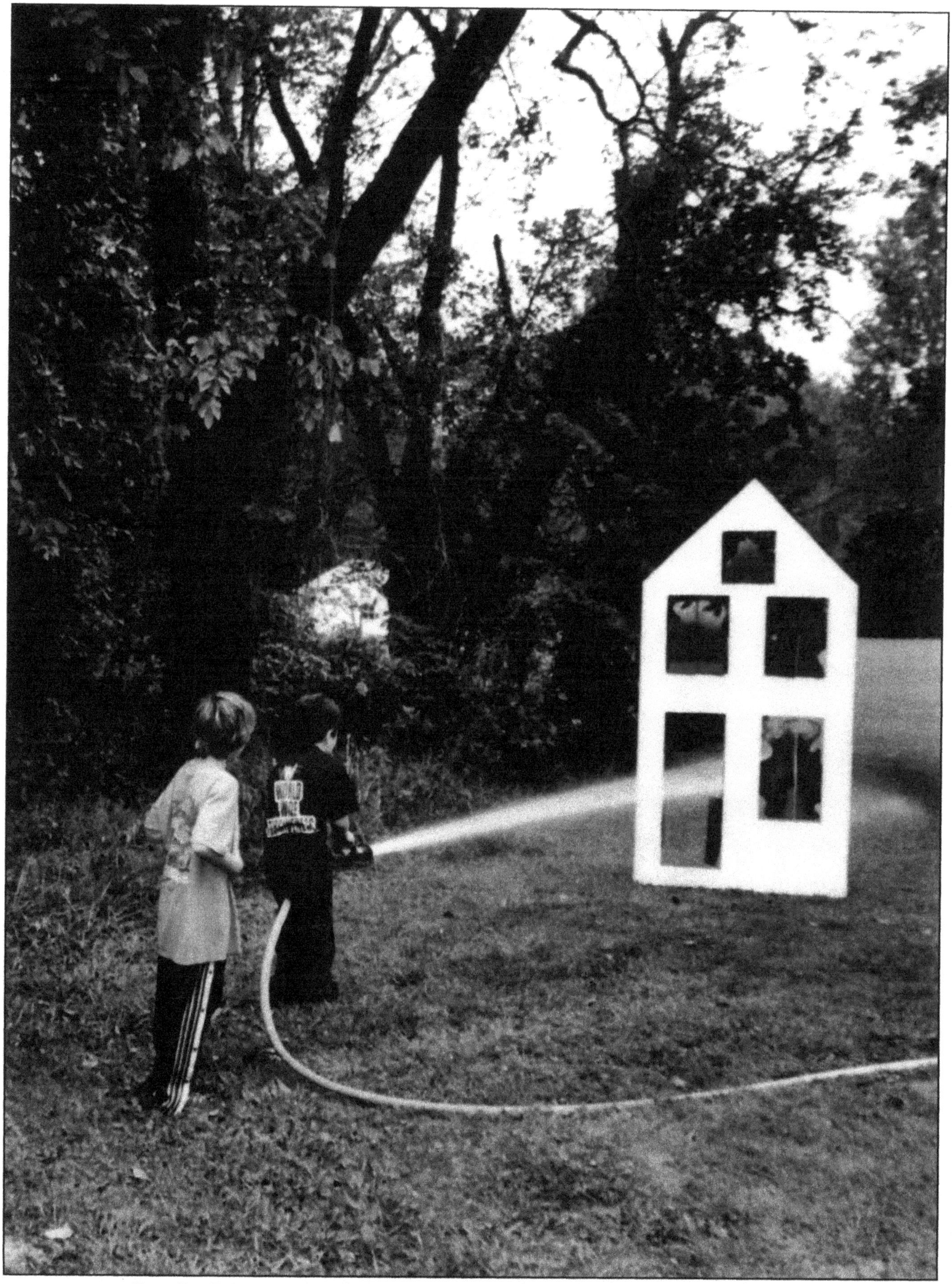

Young Fire Fighters attending the Open House show their skills in operating a hose line. (GVFD Photo)

100 Years of Statsitics

1904 100th Anniversary 2004

Glyndon Volunteer Fire Department

Major Incidents
1910 – 2003

Date	Type	Occupied By	Location	Damage
September 6, 1910	Buildings	Chautauqua Assoc.	Glyndon Park	$ 15,000
February 9, 1917	Building	Yates Ice House	Butler Road	
June, 1917	House	George P. Brown	Woodensburg	
September 2, 1928	Box Car	Western Maryland R.R.	Emory Grove	
December 8, 1929	Building	Glyndon Church	Butler Road	
June 28, 1940	Barn	M. F. J. Hoen	Glyndon	$ 4,500
April 9, 1941	House	Benson Raver	Greenspring Ave.	2,000
March 14, 1954	Barn	Thomas Bull	Baublitz Ave.	3,124
January 16, 1956	House	Gertrude Battle	St. Paul Ave.	3,300
August 4, 1956	House	W. P. Schew	Timber Grove	2,600
January 16, 1957	Barn	C. E. Williams	Longnecker Rd.	84,200
October 31, 1957	Barn	Miller Estates	Tufton Ave.	13,000
January 19, 1959	House	Warren Smith	Railroad Ave.	2,400
October 29, 1959	House	Thomas Gamber	Bowers Lane	2,300
December 15, 1959	House	James Clark	Dyer Ave.	4,000
August 14, 1960	House	Dillion Smith	Butler Rd.	5,000
November 11, 1960	Barn	Herman Hughes	Piney Grove Rd.	9,500
December 6, 1960	Barn	Dillion Smith	Butler	10,000
January 23, 1961	House	Charles Fisbaugh	Bower Lane	1,500
June 14, 1961	House	Donald Brewer	Dover Road	3,500
February 17, 1964	House	M. Beacraft	Bowers Lane	3,500
April 5, 1967	Building	Glyndon Laundry	Central Ave.	125,000
January 8, 1969	Barn	——	——	3,450
July 30, 1970	House	——	Bowers Lane	8,000
August 20, 1970	House	——	Wabash Ave.	7,000
November 25, 1970	House	——	Butler Rd.	11,000
January 16, 1972	House	——	Railroad Ave.	8,000
June 20, 1974	Diesel Locomotive	——	Railroad Ave.	4,000
October 2, 1974	House	——	Bowers Lane	4,500
October 6, 1974	House	——	Central Ave.	52,000
December 30, 1974	House	——	Bond & Central Ave.	
April 9, 1975	House	——	Bond Ave.	1,500
October 23, 1976	Barn	——	Butler Road	15,000
October 30, 1976	Shed	——	Prospect Ave.	5,000
March 23, 1977	House	——	Bond Ave.	15,200
December 15, 1977	House	——	Bowers Lane	5,000
February 18, 1979	Building	Dutterer's of Manchester	115 Main St., Manchester, Md.	
March 1, 1979	Dwelling	——	31 Fennington Circle	
April 4, 1979	Building	Majestic Distillery	Bonita & Crondall Lane	
June 23, 1979	Building	Suburban Propane	Old Hanover Rd.	
August 13, 1979	Dwelling	80 Sacred Heart Lane		70,000

Date	Type	Occupied By	Location	Damage
November 1, 1979	Building	Crab Deck	14313 Hanover Road	
July 15, 1980	Building	Foster Farms	Bonita Ave.	
August 5, 1983	5 Alarm	Shipley Transfer	Rt. 91, Finksburg, Md.	
August 7, 1983	Dwelling	Timbergrove & Timber Run		60,000
October 24, 1989	Barn	3939 Butler Road		
November 21, 1989	Building	State Roads Commission	35 Railroad Ave.	
February 26, 1990	Dwelling	103 Brookbury Drive		
March 28, 1990	Building	Universal Security	10324 S. Dolfield Ave.	
August 15, 1990	Dwelling	Reisterstown Rd.		
October 18, 1990	Apt. Dwellings	Tornado	Chartley Area	
October 27, 1990	Building	Far East Restaurant	Reisterstown Shopping Center	
March 18, 1991	Building	Painters Mill Music Fair	Music Fair Road	
June 29, 1991	Haz-Mat	Box Car on Train	Emory Grove	
August 20, 1991	Building	2nd Alarm	10840 York Road	
August 23, 1991	Dwelling	2nd Alarm	1913 Billy Barton Circle	
November 17, 1991	Building	5 Alarms	Westminster	
June 21, 1992	Building	6 Alarms–Sportsman's Hall	15391 Hanover Road	
June 23, 1992	Apt. – 2nd.	2 Families	401 Shirley Manor Road	
February 6, 1994	Dwelling	Russell Brown	1401 Knox Street	$80,000
January 8, 1995	School	Baltimore County School	Sparks Ave.	
February 5, 1995	Dwelling	——	812 Ivydale Ave.	50,000
July 21, 1995	Apartment	37 Brookbury Dr.		
December 17, 1995	Dwelling	324 Norgulf Rd.		30,000
April 25, 1996	Woods	Foster Farms	Bonita Ave.	(9,000 gals. of water)
October 10, 1996	Building	John Brown's Store	13501 Falls Rd.	
December 30, 1996	Building	Western Maryland College	239 W. Main St., Westminster	
August 13, 1997	Auto Accid. Rescue	Head-on Double Fly Out	Worthington & Sagamore	
November 17, 1997	Dwelling	Patol Vikraj	12309 Bonmot Pl.	
July 24, 1998	Dwelling 2nd Alarm	Robert Stevenson	12613 Timbergrove Rd.	
October 1, 1999	Dwelling	David Stern	21 Beecham Ct.	200,000
November 11, 1999	Auto Accid. Rescue & Fire	1 Fatality	12032 Bonita Ave.	
November 28, 1999	Dwelling	Gillet	14300 Green Rd.	
December 23, 1999	Building 5th Alarm	Goodwill Industries	79 W. Main St.	500,000
September 27, 2000	Auto Accid. Rescue	1 Fatality	100 Chartley Drive	
October 13, 2000	Auto Accid. Rescue	1 Fatality	4406 Worthington Ave.	
March 19, 2001	Gun Shot Wounds	1 Fatality – 2 Fly Outs	12210 Owings Mills Blvd.	
September 5, 2001	Dwelling	Pulte Homes	11226 Appaloosa Drive	50,000
September 11, 2001	Standby due to Terrorist Attacks on Washington, D.C. and New York City			
October 15, 2001	Investigation – Unknown Substance		9/11 Related	
October 30, 2001	Investigation – Unknown Substance		9/11 Related	
November 16, 2001	Investigation – Unknown Substance		9/11 Related	
April 13, 2002	Apt, 3 Alarms	Seigel Management	133 Willow Bend Dr.	
August 16, 2002	Dwelling		4427 Butler Road	200,000
October 15, 2002	Auto Accid. Rescue	1 Fatality – 1 Fly Out	Worthington & Timber Knoll	
January 12, 2003	Building		112 Butler Rd.	100,000
March 1, 2003	Building		2 Glyntree Garth	200,000
July 11, 2003	Building	Double stabbing	650 Glynock Place	
July 25, 2003	Building		600 Glynock Place	50,000
September 5, 2003	Auto Accid.	Fatal	Worthington Ave.	
September 10, 2003	Building		8 Pemberly Ave.	50,000
November 10, 2003	Building		3918 Log Trail Way	20,000
November 11, 2003	Auto Accid.	2 Fatalities	Tufton Ave.	
November 22, 2003	Auto Accid. Rescue	1 Fatality		

FIRE ALARM STATISTICS

The maintenance of alarm records through the early years of the department's operation was sketchy at best. No reliable, formal, records of fire alarms from the period prior to 1910 have been found. There are a number of references in the early minutes of the department to fires to which the department responded. In the early days, there seems to have been no formalized system for keeping records of alarms and the members who responded to them. In some cases the details of early fires fought by the department were gathered from published accounts in the local newspapers. The information presented here is what we know about the alarms the department responded to over the last 100 years.

It is not clear exactly when formal fire/incident reporting was initiated. The fire and incident reports prior to 1953 have been lost. As a result we only have the alarm statistics for the period 1953 through 2003. These figures do show, however, that over that 50-year period, the number of alarms has been steadily increasing as Glyndon and the surrounding community have grown

Number of Alarms by Year

Year	Alarms	Year	Alarms
1953	48	1979	461
1954	74	1980	493
1955	60	1981	538
1956	52	1982	501
1957	64	1983	438
1958	55	1984	413
1959	92	1985	378
1960	55	1986	465
1961	52	1987	434
1962	72	1988	463
1963	75	1989	490
1964	88	1990	473
1965	88	1991	511
1966	75	1992	457
1967	88	1993	533
1968	113	1994	531
1969	152	1995	608
1970	137	1996	655
1971	140	1997	636
1972	150	1998	633
1973	172	1999	728
1974	164	2000	693
1975	176	2001	645
1976	241	2002	774
1977	280	2003	849
1978	341		

The following chart shows the rapid increase in the number of alarms over the last several years graphically.

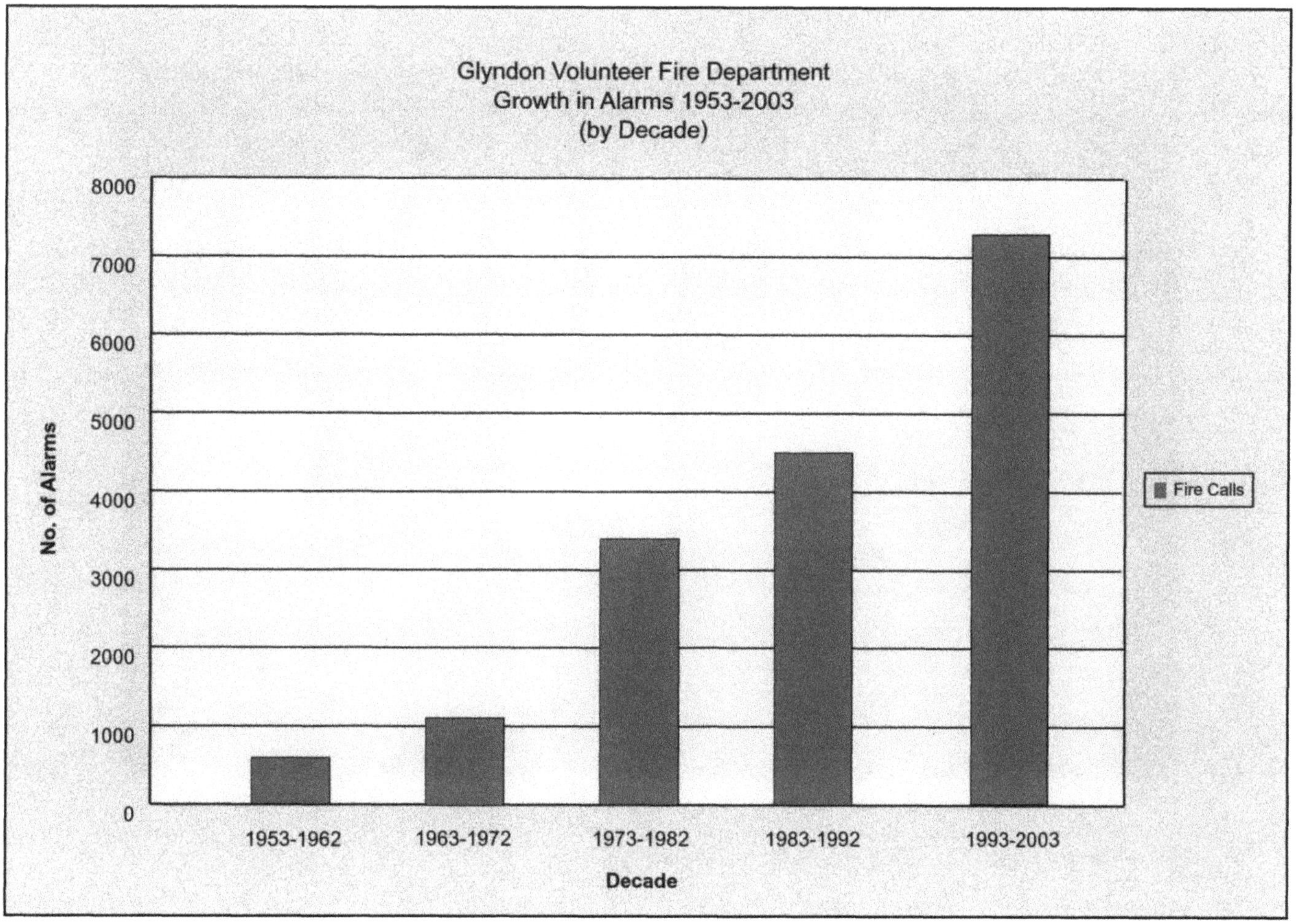

Acknowledgments

100th Anniversary Committee. Seated (L to R) Dorothy Schultz, Kathy Reitz, Rosemary Stem, Mary Merriken, Jody Gore and Joan Wolfenden. Standing (L to R) Ted Schultz, Scott Warner, J. Peter Brach, Jr., Richard Merriken, Sr., James E. Warner, Jr. and Richard Stem, Sr. (Photo by Bernard J. Roche)

The publication of "Answering the Call" is the product of the extraordinary efforts of the members of the Glyndon Volunteer Fire Department, and many of our friends and neighbors who supported this substantial effort with historical notes, photographs, and information pertinent to the department's history. To all of our members, and the people and organizations that contributed to making "Answering the Call" a definitive history of our first 100 years we extend our sincerest thanks.

A special thank you goes to the dedicated members of the 100th Anniversary Committee who labored untiringly to review 100 years of minute books, some of which were barely readable, and extract not only the significant historical information but also the small but interesting details which provide insight into the Glyndon community and its volunteer fire department. Members of the committee also reviewed and updated the material from the three earlier publications prepared in celebration of our 60th, 75th and 90th anniversaries. The members of the committee, chaired by J. Peter Brach, Jr. are: Richard Merriken, Sr., Mary Merriken, Kathy Reitz, Ted Schultz, Dorothy Schultz, Richard Stem, Sr., Rosemary Stem, James E. Warner, Jr., Scott Warner, Joan Wolfenden and Jody Gore representing the Ladies Auxiliary. Past members of the committee are Richard Stem, Jr. and Calvin Reter. Both are past chairmen. Two members of the committee, C. E. "Gene" Cole and Thomas Wolfenden, who served the committee with distinction in its early days passed away before they could enjoy the fruits of their labor.

Mitchell Warner and Dorothy Schultz provided the information that is the basis for the history of the Junior Fire department. Joan Wolfenden, Rosemary Stem and Jody Gore developed the material for the history of the Ladies Auxiliary. Marty Listwan and Kathy Reitz designed our 100th Anniversary Logo. Rosemary Stem spearheaded the effort by the 100th Anniversary Committee that resulted in the design and production of our commemorative afghan.

We wish to recognize the contribution of the Baltimore County Public Library in providing assisting us in documenting events related to the history of the department. The Reisterstown Branch was especially helpful in providing access to the Reisterstown Room collection. Rosemary Stem and Jody Gore conducted this research. The BCPL Heritage Web Site provided copies of historic photographs of Glyndon for use in "Answering the Call"

Two of our community organizations were helpful in gathering information on the history of the town of Glyndon. The Glyndon Community Association graciously allowed us to use selected excerpts from the Glyndon 100th anniversary publication "The Glyndon Story 1871-1971" by Myrtle Eckhardt in telling our story. Anne O'Neil of Historic Glyndon provided information on the Glyndon Depot fire and other significant events impacting the history of the department.

The Maryland Historical Society provided a photograph of the Great Baltimore Fire of February 1904.

Joel Woods provided a number of extraordinary photographs of our apparatus from his world-class collection of fire apparatus photographs. There are many excellent photographs in this book taken over the years by our members and others. In most cases, these photographs are from the department's archives and files could not be attributed to a particular photographer or department member. We decided to designate these photographs as coming from the "Archives" or as a "GVFD Photo." We want to recognize the work of these anonymous photographers and say thank you for their fine work.

Bernard J. Roche Photography served as the official photographer for the 100th anniversary. Creative Imaging took the 100th Anniversary Banquet pictures.

The Glyndon Volunteer Fire Department is indebted to all of our members and their families, the many people from our community, and all who helped in any way to make our 100th year a memorable one. To all of you: many, many thanks.

The publication of "Answering the Call" would have been significantly more difficult with out the publications prepared for our 60th, 75th and 90th anniversary celebrations. We drew heavily on the historical material found in these wonderful books. To recognize that work, and the people who performed it, we here add the acknowledgements from those anniversary publications just as they appeared when the books were published in 1964, 1979 and 1994

The 60th Anniversary - 1964

The Glyndon Volunteer Fire Department expresses its thanks to the following 1964 committee through whose untiring efforts this book was prepared: C. Leroy Wolfgang, J. Peter Brach, Jr., C. Eugene Cole,

100th Anniversary Logo

James E. Warner, Jr., Richard Stem, Sr., Richard Merriken and Calvin Reter.

The Company is especially indebted to C. Robert Beach, Mrs. Mary Merriken, Mrs. Norma S. Brach, Carlton Chilcoat, Norman Fritz, J. Edward Hewes, Rev. Dr. Eugene Woodward, Al Pennoni, Mrs. Mary Lauterbach, Mrs. Lilly Pierce, Mrs. Margaret Merkel and George Fritz for their invaluable assistance in the preparation of this book. Quotations that appear in the text are extracts from the minutes of the Department.

75th Anniversary - 1979

The Glyndon Volunteer Fire Department also expresses its thanks to the following 1979 committee through whose efforts this book was updated: Richard Merriken, Sr., James E. Warner, Jr., Mary K. Merriken, Richard Stem, Sr., Richard Cole and C. Leroy Wolfgang.

90th Anniversary - 1994

The Department is especially indebted to help from Irene Jackson, Marie Cole, Marty Listwan and Scott Wolfenden as well as the 90th anniversary committee of: C. E. Cole, Tom Wolfenden, Richard Stem, Jr., Richard Stem, Sr., J. E. Warner, Jr., Richard Cole, L. Thomas Johnson, Edward C. Schultz, Richard Merriken, Sr., J. P. Brach, Jr., Joan Wolfenden, Rosemary Stem, Jody Gore, Judi Stem and Carol Beimschla for the preparation of this 90th anniversary book.

J. Peter Brach, Jr., Editor
"Answering the Call"

Commemorative Afghan

Patrons

1904 100th Anniversary 2004

The Glyndon Volunteer Fire Department thanks all of our members and friends who by becoming Patrons supported our 100th Anniversary celebration.

Kristie Altomonte
Tony & Cyndi Altomonte
Douglas & Kathy Wolfenden
FF Steve Pearce, Station 29
Gladys & Ed Pearce
Elizabeth Talbert
Michael & Layna Lambert
Patricia L. Runner
Walter D. Talbert, Jr.
Russ Lessner
Kristin Warren
Jim and Maxine Warner
Jim and Kathy Warner
John and Donna Warner
Jill and David Jones
Casey and Leona Caples
The Rudow Family
Dave & Marcia Garnice
Leonard & Harriet Sonshine
The Garnice Kids
Mayo & Sally Garnice
Buck & Ida Cullum
William H. Pearson, Jr.
Howard D. Isennock, Jr.
Lurlie L. Isennock
Stuart W. Carter
Lucille Carter Colson
God Bless Those That Serve

Glyndon Vol., Thank You
We Salute Those That Serve
Pop's Littlest Angel Alec
Congrats - Jody Gore
The Sainz Family
Gene & Joan Mersinger
An Angel From Glyndon
Winfield & Jessie Abbott
Scott Wolfenden
Ashley Wolfenden
Jack & Christina Souzer
Alan & Linda Torbit
Dorothy Schultz
Edward Schultz
Expert Medical Opinions
The Lorden Family
Fullcircle Healing
J. Robet Button
George & JoAnn Albright
Memory of James Carter Family
Memory of Claudia Barnes
The Listwan's Polish Power
Randy and Anita Brown
In Memory of Margaret Brown
In Memory of Ray & Maxine Warner
CJ, Samantha, Kassidy & Amanda Reitz
Ryan and Colby Warner
Scott & Kathy Warner

Sponsors

1904 100th Anniversary 2004

DARREN BARNES

HOUSE OF LIQUORS

"Everything in Spirits, PLUS Courtesy and Service"

CARROLL PLAZA
Westminster, MD 21157

410-848-1314

ITE
Fire Apparatus
INTERSTATE TRUCK EQUIPMENT

Seagrave Aerialscope

Congratulations to the
Glyndon Volunteer Fire Department
on 100 Years of Community Service

Seagrave™

Clintonville, Wisconsin
Phone: 715-823-2141

Congratulations to the Members of the Glyndon Volunteer Fire Department for 100 Years of Dedicated Service

---

Your Complete Landscape Source

GLYNDON GARDENS

Glyndon Gardens, LLC.
205 Hanover Pike, Reisterstown, MD 21136
Tel 410-833-2791 Fax 410-833-2945

DANIEL L. CAREY

Harry O. Shaneybrook, Inc.

PLUMBING • HEATING • SEWERAGE SYSTEMS • EXCAVATING

144 WESTMINSTER RD.
REISTERTOWN, MD 21136

PHONE 410-833-3820
410-833-0200
FAX 410-833-4459

Delmarva Fire Apparatus

5403 MT. HOLLY ROAD
EAST NEW MARKET, MD 21631
410-476-3785 • FAX 410-221-1640
www.delmarvafire.com

STEVEN R. BEAVERS and RICHARD F. BEAVERS
Cell: 410-463-0776 Cell: 410-463-0777

Beaverbuilt Equipment

Congratulations
On
100 Years of Service

Pete and Norma Brach
Joe, Jan, Becky and Scott Brach
Norman, Yvonne, Ivy and Forest Brach
Ted and Ann Vedock

Dancer Lucy Gracie

In Memoriam

William H. Reter
And
Susie R. Reter
Co-founder of the Glyndon Volunteer Fire Department
Ladies Auxiliary

By
Calvin and James Reter

Congratulations on your 100th Anniversary
And
In Memory of Thomas H. Wolfenden, Jr.
By
His wife Joan, Children: Barb and Steve Mack, Debbie and Mark Riss, Thomas Scott and Pattie Wolfenden, Doug and Kathy Wolfenden, his Grandchildren and Great Grandson

Congratulations on your 100th Anniversary
and
In loving Memory of our Pop-Pop
Thomas H. Wolfenden, Jr.
1931-2000

Eric, Albina and Alec Parks, Mindy Parks, Sara and Kendra Mack, Amy and Mike Caouette, Dan Riss, Jessica Spriggs, Scott Wolfenden and Ashley Wolfenden

Congratulations on your 100th Anniversary

Mary and Richard Merriken, Sr.
Gloria and Richard Merriken, Jr.
Jessica, Samuel, Joey and Caitlyn Conver
Ronnie, Kimberly and Jackson Merriken
Jeremy Blake Houck Tennant
Randall, Gail, Tiffany and Jeremy Merriken
Daniel Felton and Brian Funk

Congratulations
to the
Glyndon Volunteer Fire Department
On your
100th Year Anniversary

Best wishes from the

Ladies Auxiliary of the Glyndon V. F. D.

Congratulations on 100 Years
of
Service to the Community

Your Friends From Across the Bridge

Reisterstown Volunteer Fire Company, Inc.

Congratulations
and
Best Wishes
for
Continued Success in the Next 100

Boring Volunteer Fire Company, Inc.
Organized 1907

Cockeysville Volunteer Fire Company
Established in 1896

Our Officers and Members
Welcome the
Glyndon Volunteers into the 100 Year Club

Congratulations

Elwood H. Banister, President
Kevin Roberts, Chief

Congratulations on 100 Years of Dedicated Service to the Community!

The Officers and Members of the Owings Mills Volunteer Fire Company

The Officers, Members, Ladies Auxiliary,
and Junior Fire Brigade of
The Community Volunteer Fire Department of
Bowley's Quarters and Vicinity, Inc.
Congratulates the

Glyndon Volunteer Fire Department

On their celebration of 100 Years
of dedicated service to the citizens of
Glyndon and Baltimore County

North Point Edgemere
Baltimore County
We Do It All
Fire Rescue-Marine
260

Congratulations
on your
100 year anniversary!

Officers and Members
of the
Reese and Community Volunteer Fire Company

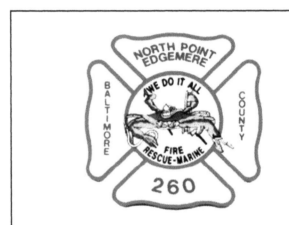

INDEX

Printed in the USA
CPSIA information can be obtained
at www.ICGtesting.com
JSHW072021140824
68134JS00042B/3725

9 781681 621951